The Mystic Shift

Christianity Beyond Religion

CODY ROTHWELL

Mt 22:38-40

The Center for Divine Encounter

Dedication

THIS BOOK is dedicated to the mystics of the past,
whose passion for knowing God drove them deeper
into Divine relationship, a depth no creed, doctrine or religion
could attain alone. This includes my great-grandmother,
Anna Iverson, my grandpa, Campbell Iverson,
and my grandmother Gladys Iverson,
who were all extremely influential
in the unleashing of my spiritual fervor.

Contents

Acknowledgements vi

Foreword I viii

Foreword II xi

Introduction 1

1 From Sinner to Vessel: How We View Ourselves 29

2 Judgment to Love: How We View Others 43

3 From Concept to Mystery: How We View God 53

4 From Belief to Liberation: How We View Salvation 63

5 From Disobedience to Opportunity: How We View Sin 81

6 From Fear to Faith: How We View the Unknown 95

7 From Paradise to Presence: How We View Heaven and Earth 109

8 From Closed Book to Open Revelation: How We View
   God's Word 121

9 From Building to Assembly: How We View Church 143

10 From Conversion to Awakening: How We View the
   Great Commission 157

Epilogue 177

About the Author 179

Acknowledgements

I WOULD LIKE TO THANK my editors, Cory Rothwell, Krista Rothwell, and Brian Sherburne. You guys have been my second (and third, fourth and fifth!) pair of eyes. I have so appreciated your feedback and insights.

I would like to thank Ziya Laura, a former student of mine, for designing the cover of this book. Her artistry and creative expression will manifest much abundance in her life!

I would like to thank Chelsea Farleigh who took my portrait for this book. You are a true master of photography!

I would like to thank Reverend Andrew Shykofsky and Reverend Mark Phillips who wrote forwards for this book. You both have been extremely influential in my spiritual journey. Your hearts for the spiritual life have inspired me significantly.

I would like to thank all of my former pastors and family members who helped guide me spiritually and gave me a great appreciation for the Christian tradition. This includes but is not limited to Brad Carlson, Joe Richardson, Gladys Iverson, Michael Iverson, Sharon Iverson, Lillian Iverson, Bob Iverson and Bob Frivold.

I would like to thank my parents, Steve and Darlene Rothwell, for raising me, for teaching me how to be responsible, kind and caring, and for providing me opportunities to excel. You are the best parents one could ask for, and I love you!

I would like to thank my siblings, Cory, Cami, Cali, and Coby for being my best friends throughout this life. I love you guys!

I would like to thank my in-laws, Joel and Lisa Smith, Jim and Sally Burgoyne, Deanna Horsley, Josiah Smith, and Chelsea Farleigh for accepting me into your awesome family. You've been a constant support to us and our daughters.

I would like to thank my two beautiful daughters, Eily and Emmy, for making me a dad. You have taught me to be present and how to love unconditionally. I dedicate my life to you. You both mean everything to me, and I love you so much!

Last, but certainly not least, I would like to thank my beautiful wife Krista for loving me and supporting me in this book-writing journey. I love you so much. You mean the whole world to me!

Foreword I

IT IS UNCOMMON to find individuals who are willing to question their religion and face the risk that much of what they were taught may be incomplete or untrue. Many of us grew up being taught what to believe about God, life and death and were definitely not encouraged to examine those beliefs critically.

It is much more common that people simply fade away from their religion when it is convenient to do so. When the pressure to attend regular services lessens (generally when a person ventures off to college or moves out of the family home) the grip of obligation loosens and it marks an end to much of their prior religious life. I have encountered scores of people who have stories like this.

A few very rare seekers have an insatiable desire for Truth which makes the void created by their religious upbringing unbearable. In simple terms, these souls have to know. We (and I include myself in this category) need a roadmap to help us grow spiritually, having realized that scripture could only take us so far. We crave real life experiences as a way to know with certainty what the foundation of a mature and healthy spiritual life is.

Cody Rothwell is one of these curious souls. He reached out to me in early 2021 seeking spiritual guidance. He had come across the Mystical Church of Christ website and wanted to connect. I founded the Mystical Church in 2013 following 8 years of rigorous training in a mystical Christian Order.

Through our interactions, Cody shared chapters of this book with me not long after we first connected. I was very surprised by his ability to capture the essence of the mystical approach to spirituality.

There are, of course, many great books to be found on the subject and these can generate tremendous excitement for the individual who is seeking Truth. But in the end the Narrow Gate eludes the lone mavericks; the ego, the cares of the world, one's pride and fear, one's laziness and other unforeseen obstacles rear themselves and the sincere seeker finds the Way to be unclear. Here is where having a Teacher accelerates growth one hundredfold.

Cody was quick to express an interest in being taught directly and I was moved by his fiery desire for growth. In the meantime he shared more of his book with me. As I read the chapters, I found the way he structured his material to be very fresh and engaging. He presents a traditional Christian perspective or belief and then invites the reader to explore it from a mystical angle. The tone of his writing was and is extremely engaging! Within the anecdotes and points, he expresses a deep love for God and his passion for Truth is evident.

This text offers readers who wish to question their traditional religious upbringing a chance to reevaluate their beliefs but do so while still loving God, Christ and all people. It does not seek to debunk Christianity but instead offers insights that liberate the confused Christian or spiritual seeker of any background for that matter. As you read this book, you will feel uplifted. Things that may not have sat with you despite your inclination to believe them before can now be explored in a safe and encouraging environment.

I believe reading this book will inspire readers to become confident in examining for themselves what it means to be spiritually awake and not to be afraid to question the teachings of Jesus until they can experience the profound Truth of Christ directly. It takes bravery (and quite a bit of time in meditation!) to be able to allow the scales from one's eyes to fall. What new mystics discover has the tendency to disrupt the foundation of how they have been living. It is the inner equivalent of the destruction of the temple that Jesus spoke of shortly before his crucifixion. The temple of false beliefs must crumble, every last stone, in order that the Truth may rise up from within.

Cody does a fine job of guiding the reader to those very gates that lead from falsehood to truth, never imposing a dogmatic narrative designed to force your transformation prematurely. Instead he encourages you to consider how a mystical view of the Gospels may be the very aspect of spirituality that your soul has longed for. It is up to each one to decide to pass through when they feel ready.

—Reverend Andrew Shykofsky

Foreword II

Heaven is my throne, and the earth is my footstool.
What kind of house will you build for me, says the
Lord, or what is the place of my rest? (Acts 7:49)

I MET CODY about ten years ago while pastoring a church in southwest Washington State. Throughout my ministry I tried to offer concerts once a quarter. Sometimes they were outdoors, sometimes in our sanctuary. Sometimes they included a picnic, sometimes they were for Christmas or another holiday. Cody's family and singing group Anna's Kin ministered for us more than once. He and his wife provided special music for my retirement service.

Always open, inquisitive, and friendly, I took to him and his family right away. As we got to know one another I realized our paths had taken a similar arc. It is that arc, or shift, which Cody presents in *The Mystic Shift*.

For me it is a shift from formal doctrine-based spirituality to one that nurtures loving relationship. It moves from locating spiritual experience in a *place* to a *person*. It moves faith in a book to trusting the Christ about whom that book speaks.

More than once, I have heard people speak about being done with "organized religion." I confess my response was often a cynical "would you prefer *disorganized* religion?" But I did understand the heart of the statement. There are many who have been wounded within the institutional church, and that transcends denomination or religious expression. I also have felt the wounds of living in a bubble where we were always measuring our spiritual accomplishments. People would talk about going to "the next level" instead of expressing contentment in simply experiencing God. But, as one of the wounded, I did my share of wounding as well.

I agree with Cody, it is time for a Mystic Shift. This is what Stephen was saying when he quoted Isaiah 61:1: "Thus says the Lord: 'Heaven is my throne and the earth is my footstool; what is the house that you would build for me, and what is my resting place?'" My loose paraphrase would be, "Do you really think you can build a place to contain me, the living God?"

Stephen had been arrested for preaching the Good Story about Jesus, the message that God had forgiven the world in Christ. He did not speak of doctrines and fundamental beliefs. Indeed, the book of Acts says he was "full of grace and power" and that those who argued with him "could not withstand the wisdom and the Spirit with which he spoke." (Acts 7:8,10)

His understanding had shifted from a narrow view that God was known through ritual, law and location to the broad and universal message that God showed us in Christ. Unsurprisingly, this got him a lot of trouble. He was arrested and brought before the High Priest.

Instead of arguing doctrine, Stephen began a long speech outlining the history of God's relationship with Israel. It is near the end that he asks the same question that Isaiah did, "What kind of house will you build for me?" The priests must have known the next verse of Isaiah 66:2 "All these things my hand has made, and so all these things are mine, says the Lord. But this is the one to whom I will look, to the humble and contrite in spirit, who trembles at my word." God doesn't want a structure; he wants to enliven our spirits with His presence in all things.

The authorities did not receive this well. Though they had seen Stephen's face light up like an angel (Acts 6:15), they chose death instead of life, his death. They dragged him outside the city and began to stone him. All that was on Stephen's mind was Jesus; "Lord Jesus, receive my spirit." All that was on his heart was the echo of Christ's words: "Lord do not hold this sin against them."

Stephen discovered something beyond religious ritual or dusty doctrines; he discovered life. And so may we. To do so, perhaps Cody will allow me to use a deeply theological word: Eclectic.

I have learned to find Christ in every denominational expression. I have taken wisdom from Roman Catholics, Orthodox, Quakers, Mainline Protestants, Progressives and Evangelicals. I have experienced Christ in my chihuahua Kitty, in the laugh of a child, in conversation over a beer and in the hummingbirds sipping the nectar from our feeder. And, not to be too much of an iconoclast, I have also discovered Christ in the lives of the Ancients, even among those outside the traditional Christian faith.

I encourage you to read this book deeply. I appreciate people like Cody, who do not have an axe to grind, but rather desire for our hearts to be open to the wooing of the Spirit within our everyday lives. May the grace and peace of Jesus be upon you as you read.

—Reverend Mark Phillips

Introduction

THIS BOOK HAS taken me ten years to write. The principles described in this book have been learned, lived and internalized. They are more true to me now than when *The Mystic Shift* was first initiated in my life. Finally, God has given me the motivation to put words to these principles.

My name is Cody Rothwell, and I am an advocate of Christian mysticism. My career is as a middle school teacher, but my true passion lies in Christian spirituality.

I come from a very spiritually-minded family. My great-grandmother, Anna Iverson, was a giant of faith. Her relationship with God grew in the midst of fifteen years of great turmoil. As her circumstances worsened, her faith in God grew. Because of it, she became a vessel of healing and transformation. Her son Campbell, my grandpa, was an alcoholic by the age of fourteen and dropped out of the eighth grade. Every morning he would wake up, go out to the barn, and take a couple swigs of moonshine before milking the cows. He would continue drinking throughout the day and quickly established himself as the town drunk. He was even given the nickname "Half-Pint Cam" by community members on account of the amount of alcohol he could consume on a daily basis. His alcoholism soon led to destructive behavior. He picked fights with random strangers on the street, and people feared walking on the same side of the street as him. He cursed others, including his own mother who desperately prayed for his liberation. He smoked excessively, robbed the neighbor's houses, and stole the neighbor's farm animals. He was arrested on numerous occasions, and he was eventually sentenced to one to five years at Monroe Correctional Facility. His downward spiral continued for years without a light of hope. He was desperate to change, but his self-affliction ran deep and prevented him from escaping his suffering. Then one day the Spirit moved him, and he gave his life over completely to God. Within four days of his surrender, he gave up drinking, fighting, cursing, smoking, and stealing. He was liberated of his torment, and he made a vow to tell the story of his salvation whenever and wherever he could in case his story would help somebody else who was going through a similar struggle. Decades later he became the pastor of a small congregation in McKenna, Washington that grew by the hundreds. He was never ordained by a university or a church, but as God told him, "I ordain you." Campbell became a mentor to many, and through his ministry he witnessed countless spiritual liberations amongst his beloved congregants. Those that knew him knew him by his love.

I personally never knew my grandpa. He died when I was a year old. My mother would tell me stories; how he used to take me out to pick raspberries and watch the chickens; how he used to pray over me, and I would refer to him as "Pa." Besides those stories, I am only left with the memories told to me by various relatives and community members about his passion for God and his heart for others.

After my grandpa died, my parents moved in with my grandma. My grandma was a very righteous woman. Strict in her discipline, she would always correct us should we veer off a respectable course. If we harmed a mouse or shot at a bird, she would scold us. If we said "gosh" or "jeez," she would slap our mouths. She told us they were slang for God and Jesus, neither word we were supposed to use in vain (which at the time we understood to mean cussing). Yet, beneath the layer of strictness she exhibited, she loved us unconditionally. No matter what we did, she would give us a big hug and tell us how much she loved us. She would anoint us with oil, and pray over us every day. My grandma was religious, but her relationship with

God was deeper than religion. Had it not been for my grandma, I do not think I would have been interested in spirituality. When I turned six years old, my grandma gave me my first Bible. I still have that Bible, and every time I see it I am reminded of her relationship with God. When I began grade school, my

> Christianity is not a religion or a philosophy, but a relationship and a lifestyle. The core of that lifestyle is thinking of others as Jesus did, instead of ourselves.
>
> RICK WARREN

grandma began to prophesy over me. I remember her words, said to me over and over again: "Cody, you are going to be a pastor someday like your grandpa." This had a profound impact on me, giving me a sense of a spiritual calling. I embodied grandma's words, imagining I was already a pastor. Not only did I believe in the prophecy, but others believed it too. They encouraged me in this calling, and I only grew more passionate. Over the following years, grandma gave me grandpa's traveling communion set and his prayer room, the sacred building he went to communicate with God and write his sermons. I knew of the sacredness of this place, and I continued to treat it as such. I used to write pamphlets in the prayer room for "my church" and had a mission to bring family and friends to this church (though the prayer room was tiny!). During those years, I remember signing my name "Pastor Cody Rothwell" on birthday and Christmas cards. Others found this quite amusing! I remember serving communion and constantly praying over others. At the age of seven I was baptized, and my spiritual fervor was unleashed. A passion began to burn within my heart for the things of God, and growing my relationship with God became the driving force of my life.

When I started middle school, I became very involved with my church's youth group. I drew extremely close to the youth pastor and his wife, both of whom I greatly admired for their spiritual fervor. The pastor was well aware of my pastoral calling, for my grandma told him of my prophecy before I even started attending youth group. I also admired several of the high school youth leaders. One in particular became my mentor and encouraged me to join the worship team as a piano player. He taught me how to play chords, how to use the foot pedal, and how to balance my sound with the rest of the worship team. As the years went on my piano skills improved, and I was being asked to play for the entire church congregation. My grandma attended these services, and I remember her smiling at me as I played. I continued my involvement with the church throughout middle and high school and grew in both musical ability and spiritual maturity.

During my senior year in high school I plateaued spiritually. While I was still involved with the church, I knew that God was calling me elsewhere. The Assembly was instrumental in my spiritual development and justified my calling to be a pastor. It was the Assembly where I learned how to open my heart for God's direction.

In 2006 I graduated from high school and left my hometown, moving to Seattle to begin my collegiate studies at Seattle Pacific University. I had been accepted to four colleges, two of which were Christian universities: Northwest University and Seattle Pacific University. My original plan was to go to Northwest University, because my pastor graduated from there and spoke highly of his experience. Nevertheless, I had several relatives who attended Seattle Pacific University (SPU), all of whom were later involved in some form of ministry. SPU also offered me the best financial package, so I chose to attend SPU.

During my first year at SPU I had two major spiritual revelations. The first revelation happened when I opened up my Bible and read Matthew 22:36-40. I had read this passage numerous times before, but for some reason reading it this time the Spirit spoke through. In the passage, Jesus responded to his disciples' question asking what the greatest commandment in the law was. Jesus replied:

*'Love the Lord your God with all your heart and with all your soul
and with all your mind.' This is the first and greatest commandment.
And the second is like it: 'Love your neighbor as yourself.' All the Law
and the Prophets hang on these two commandments.*

All the law and the prophets hang on the commandment of love.
"How fascinating!" I thought. After reading this passage, I was then
led to turn to 1 John 4:8. As John the Evangelist writes:

Whoever does not love does not know God, because God is love.

God *is* love, which means that love *is* God. "How revolutionary!" I said
to myself. I was then led to the thirteenth chapter of Paul's letter to the
Corinthians, and the gospel message became clear to me:

*If I speak in the tongues of men or of angels, but do not have love,
I am only a resounding gong or a clanging cymbal. If I have the gift
of prophecy and can fathom all mysteries and all knowledge, and if
I have a faith that can move mountains, but do not have love, I am
nothing. If I give all I possess to the poor and give over my body to
hardship that I may boast, but do not have love, I gain nothing.*

*Love is patient, love is kind. It does not envy, it does not boast,
it is not proud. It does not dishonor others, it is not self-seeking, it is
not easily angered, it keeps no record of wrongs. Love does not delight
in evil but rejoices with the truth. It always protects, always trusts,
always hopes, always perseveres.*

*Love never fails. But where there are prophecies, they will cease;
where there are tongues, they will be stilled; where there is knowledge,
it will pass away. For we know in part and we prophesy in part, but
when completeness comes, what is in part disappears. When I was a
child, I talked like a child, I thought like a child, I reasoned like a child.
When I became a man, I put the ways of childhood behind me. For now
we see only a reflection as in a mirror; then we shall see face to face.
Now I know in part; then I shall know fully, even as I am fully known.*

*And now these three remain: faith, hope and love. But the greatest
of these is love.*

The Spirit revealed an important truth to me through the reading of these three passages: *love* is the greatest of all Christian actions. You can have all the knowledge of the scriptures; you can have the gift of prophecy and perform wonders and miracles; you can even have faith that can move the mountains, but if you do not love you are nothing and do not know God. It does not matter your religion, the church you attended, your political stance, your race, your culture, your social class, your gender, your sexual orientation, or your past. The greatest indicator of a Christian is love. When I realized this I lamented, for I knew that love wasn't the image of Christians to most outsiders. In fact, love was not even the image of a Christian to most Christians! Something was seriously wrong.

My second revelation happened when I was reading C.S. Lewis's book *Mere Christianity*. In one of the chapters Lewis talks about the vices that separate the soul from God. According to Lewis, pride is the complete anti-God state of mind. One is not separated from God because one fails to uphold some religious rule. Shoot, Jesus constantly broke religious rules. One is not separated from God for failing to go to church, forgetting to read the Bible, drinking, smoking, or having premarital sex. One is not separated from God for being gay, getting an abortion or being a democrat or a republican. One is not separated from God for exploring other faiths or being tolerant of other viewpoints. No, *pride* is what separates us from God. *Pride* is what led to Lucifer's fall from heaven. *Pride* is what led to man's removal from the Garden of Eden. *Pride* has caused civilizations and empires to fall again and again.

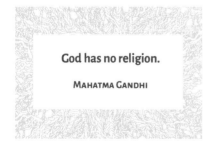

God has no religion.

MAHATMA GANDHI

The greatest barrier between man and God, barricading man from divine connection, is pride. Pride incarcerates the soul in its own arrogance, expanding the ego to where love cannot pass through. All sins stem from this vice of pride. I want to be clear with you, my reader, for it took me years to learn this truth and come to a spiritual breakthrough: there is no Godly pride. By seeing pride for what it really was, I began to separate from my religion. This created a massive space within me that only God could fill, and this space only called me deeper.

In 2010, I overcame the last of the religious barriers that kept me separate from God. I entered a state of depression, what I considered my dark night of the soul. I was stuck in a world of gray. Nothing excited me. Nothing moved me. Frankly, everything sucked. I was not suicidal, but I felt I was in purgatory. None of my religious practices alleviated my suffering. Reading the Bible failed to uplift me. I felt fake going to church. Even my prayers seemed to fall on deaf ears. I felt God had completely abandoned me. My ego fought to stay relevant in this dark space, and the fight created an immense amount of suffering. Finally, after four months, my ego gave up the fight. My old identity had died, and I felt I was nothing.

Then, in the silence and space of my nothingness, a voice radiated out. At first faint but becoming louder it said: BE PRESENT WITH ME. Upon hearing that voice, I was planted on a seat of peace. Though it lasted only for a moment, it was all I needed. As time went on, I became more present, and as my presence grew my relationship with God grew. I came to experience the unthinkable, the un-feelable, and the un-sensible depths of God, and it was here I could rest my vessel. No doctrine or theology could lead the soul to this place. After letting go of my former self, God took command of my vessel and began the process of transformation.

I quickly started to cultivate my newfound relationship with God. I still encountered God in Christianity, but I also encountered God in other religions. This led me to study Eastern and Indigenous religions and I picked up various spiritual practices, primarily Zen meditations and yoga. I also studied the human mind and human behavior, which only deepened my understanding of God. I still classified myself as a

Christian, because I had experienced God's power through following the teachings of Jesus. But I had changed, and it was difficult for me to find a church that understood God as I now did.

On February 21, 2016, six years after my spiritual reconfiguration, I was reassured of my calling as a Christian leader. Attending a church service in Longview, Washington, there was a guest preacher in attendance. Towards the end of his sermon he began to prophesy over various members in the congregation. After prophesying over two people, he turned and pointed in my direction and said, "You, with the hat." My first response was disbelief. I looked around to see who this man was pointing to, and I quickly realized I was the one wearing the hat! I had no idea what this man was going to say, but I was intrigued and kept my heart and mind open. This is what he said to me:

> You have an apostolic gift on you. There's an apostolic
> role on you. I feel like you're like Paul, the Apostle Paul,
> which is freaky because you know he's got thorns and whips
> and torture, but don't, no (*at this point there were laughs in
> the audience*). He sees the Lord. He's the 13th apostle. He
> encounters the Lord and sees Him, hears from Him, so I feel
> like the Lord, He's going to open Himself to you, yeah. There's
> open, so that John 1:51 word where you're encountering the
> Lord if you'll go after Him. So there was resistance in Paul's
> life, and I don't know anything about you. I know in my own
> life I have resisted the Lord several times, but if you stop
> resisting, the Lord will break through. The Lord will release, so
> there's an apostolic. Apostolic is leadership; it's government;
> it's a significant deal and I think it's on you. It's Cody, right?
> So Father, we pray for Cody. We lift him up to you. Release
> the apostolic in his life, Father, the things of Paul that you
> want him to walk through. There's a Timothy in his life.
> There's someone he will pour into. It may be years from now,
> Father. There's someone else coming along. We pray, Father,

give him eyes to see. I see. I almost hear that language, as I follow Christ; *follow me as I follow Christ.* Father, will you just anoint Cody with an insight into your will. Paul was a writer. Paul saw things. Paul, yeah, he endured things. So give him a spirit of endurance, but release the vision that Paul had into Cody's life I pray.

Amen.

Remarkably, years before I met my wife she was driving along the highway and heard a male voice call her name. "Krista." At first she thought it was coming from the radio. She immediately turned the radio down, and continued driving. Then she heard it

> In every religion there is love, yet love has no religion.
>
> Rumi

again. "Krista. You are going to be a pastor's wife." Coincidence or not, how the pieces of the puzzle fell together was fascinating!

Five years have passed since that prophecy, and my heart has been on fire for ministry ever since. In 2020, I felt the urge to begin writing about my spiritual journey and the truths I had learned, and the book you are reading now is the result.

Religion vs. Relationship

I have given my testimony, and I would now like to delve into the spiritual contents of this book.

Years ago my mother and I went up to Seattle to visit my great-uncle Bob Iverson. Bob was one of the more influential spiritual mentors in my youth. He and his wife, Maggie, were traveling pastors. For decades they ministered in song and sermon. Uncle Bob was an accordionist, pianist, and vocalist and Aunt Maggie played the upright bass and sang.

Aunt Maggie had passed years before, and my mother and I made it an intention to visit uncle Bob from time to time. Uncle Bob would always give us words of wisdom whenever we came to visit. During this one particular visit, Bob told us something that I will never forget: "In all my years of ministry, I have come to learn one thing: Christianity is not about religion, it is about relationship."

Now, I grew up hearing this same saying, *"Christianity is not about religion, it is about relationship,"* so it was not anything new to me. But coming from Uncle Bob struck me differently. Bob was an old-school Pentecostal preacher, devout in his religion. When he told us that Christianity was not about religion but about relationship, I was reassured of a truth I had come to discover years earlier: proclaiming yourself a Christian does not guarantee you have a relationship with God.

"Blasphemy!" I can hear the mumbles. Let me elaborate.

Below you will find a chart comparing a religious Christian to that of a relational Christian. Note: I created this chart based on my own Christian experience, where I once identified as a religious Christian and experienced the shift to a relational Christian.

Religious Christian	Relational Christian
Doctrine-driven	Love-driven
Single perspective	Open to other perspectives
One interpretation of the Bible	Open to various interpretations of the Bible
Critical of new ideas and revelations	Open to new ideas and revelations
Fixed beliefs	Evolving beliefs
Desire to convert	Desire to understand

Religious Christians hold tightly to specific Biblical interpretations and doctrines that support their particular viewpoint. Unless a Christian's internal grounds are shaken, there is likely very little movement away from these doctrines. Any new ideas or revelations are subject to these doctrines. If they do not align, they are quickly discarded. Religious Christians have a strong desire to convert others to their particular belief system.

On the other side of the spectrum are relational Christians. Relational Christians are driven by love. They value relationships above all else and are willing to sacrifice their own doctrines in the moment if it means growing in love. They are open to multiple perspectives, therefore their beliefs are continuously evolving. Relational Christians are less concerned with converting others but rather seek to understand others' differences and find value in those differences.

All Christians fall somewhere on the religion-relationship spectrum. Some lean towards religion, while others lean towards relationship. Most of us are somewhere between.

Christianity is not about religion; it is about relationship.

We hear it said often, but do we *really* believe it? How is it that Christians remain unmoved while people are leaving the church by the millions? If we truly valued relationship over religion, do not you think Christians would do something about this modern exodus instead of casting blame on the departed? As Albert Einstein once said:

Insanity is doing the same thing over and over and expecting different results.

If a Christian is given the option to either love or to keep to their religion, how likely is it that the Christian chooses love over their religion? From what I have come to experience amongst my Christian affiliates is that many of them, if not most of them, will choose to stick to their religion and let people who are disgruntled walk right out the door and then

Love is my religion.

ZIGGY MARLEY

condemn them later for falling away. I think Jesus would have responded differently. Jesus would have left the 99 conformed and followed after the stray. Jesus would have sat next to the disgruntled sheep, put his arm around them and tell them how much he loves them. It is a travesty that Jesus' very name is being used to promote doctrinal position. What arrogance! This has been the deception going on for thousands of years. It is time for a major change in how we practice Christianity.

An Introduction to Christian Mysticism

What is *the mystic shift*? And what does it have to do with Christianity?

To teach you *the mystic shift*, I think it would be helpful to first take a look at the word *mysticism*.

To some people, mysticism has something to do with magic. To others, mysticism implies mysterious realms. Still others associate mysticism with some kind of New Age spirituality.

In a way, all three of these associations are right. Mysticism can certainly be viewed as magical. According to the Merriam-Webster dictionary, magic means *an extraordinary power or influence seemingly from a supernatural source*. Any supernatural influence can therefore be called magic. Miracles, healings, the foretelling of prophecies, and the casting out of demons can all be classified as magic. Moses used magic to bring the ten plagues upon Egypt after Pharaoh refused his call to release the Hebrews from slavery. Moses also used magic to part the Reed Sea (not Red Sea; the translation of *yam suph* actually means "sea of reeds"). The Old Testament prophets used magic to foretell the coming invasions of the great Mesopotamian empires of Assyria and Babylon. Jesus used magic to feed 5,000 people with only five loaves of bread and two fish, and he also used magic to raise Lazarus from the dead, like the prophet Elijah did to the widow's son thousands of years earlier. All were supernatural acts, so all were magic. Nonetheless, I do not like to use the word "magic" to identify supernatural phenomena. Instead, I will refer to positive supernatural phenomena as God, Christ, the Holy Spirit, Love or Light, and I will refer to negative supernatural phenomena (what can also be called black magic) as the Great Egoic Consciousness (more to be said on this in chapter 2).

Mysticism can also be associated with mystery. The word *mysticism* is derived from the Greek word *müō*, which means to conceal, and its derivative *mystikos*, which means "an initiate". In the ancient world, a mystic was an initiate into a mystery religion where the initiate learned ancient spiritual knowledge. As the word found its way into Christianity, it became known as the spiritual pathway to know and experience the mysterious presence of God through Christ. As the mystic progresses deeper and deeper into this mystery, the line between human and God shrinks and the two become nearly indistinguishable. This is why mysticism can be associated with mystery.

Mysticism also contributes to what many believe is a global spiritual awakening. The mystical path is relatively new for many Western spiritual seekers, even appearing New Age to some. Mystics are seldom studied in American churches, especially in Protestant circles. After the Protestant Reformation, the mystical path was mostly forgotten about. Mysticism, however, is not only an ancient spiritual pathway but it has also been practiced within Christianity since its beginnings. In fact, mysticism can arguably be considered the oldest Christian pathway. All Abrahamic religions (Judaism, Christianity, and Islam) arose from the mystical relationship between its founders (Abraham/Moses, Jesus/Paul, Mohammed) and God. These founders wished to teach their followers how to develop this same mystical relationship with God. While some of their followers did focus on developing this mystical relationship with

God, most chose to glorify their teachers over their teachings, creating religions based on their names and casting aside any possibility of having the same human-divine relationship that their teachers possessed. The mystic founders soon became separated from their followers, achieving Godlike status in the minds of the religions based on them, which prevented many of their followers from striving to be like them. This is especially true in Christianity, where the personhood of Jesus was worshipped and his teachings were largely ignored. Nevertheless, mysticism survived in pockets of Christianity up until this day. Today, Christians are rediscovering mysticism as a legitimate and holy Christian pathway.

A Definition of Mysticism

The Merriam-Webster dictionary describes mysticism as *the experience of mystical union or direct communion with ultimate reality.* A second definition describes mysticism as *the belief that direct knowledge of God, spiritual truth, or ultimate reality can be attained through subjective experience.* Mysticism, therefore, can be understood as a spiritual pathway where the mystic's primary focus is on deepening their relationship with the Divine. While a mystic may be associated with an established religion, a mystic desires to bridge themselves directly to the Source. In short, anybody who desires to connect to God directly is a mystic.

A History of Christian Mysticism

Mysticism has long been part of the Christian tradition. Jesus was a mystic teacher (rabbi) who taught his followers how to enter the kingdom of God. He taught using various parables in his attempt to describe this mysterious kingdom, though his followers still had a difficult time understanding. He modeled the Spirit of this kingdom through numerous supernatural works, which drastically increased his influence. Jesus' relationship with God was profound and a mystery in itself. It was deeper than that of the religious leaders of his day. This put him at dangerous odds with his own religion. The leaders accused Jesus of blasphemy numerous times. They accused him of straying from what they deemed righteous behavior, of creating disorder in the crowds, and even accused him of being possessed by the ruler of all demons (Luke 11:15). Nevertheless, Jesus continued his call to bring God to all. As a result of his nonconformity, the leaders in both institutions (religious and political) sentenced him to death by crucifixion. Nailed to the cross, Jesus gave his life and initiated the awakening of a new spiritual consciousness amongst his followers.

After his death, Jesus' disciples spread his name and message around the world, making more disciples in the process. Becoming a disciple of Jesus came with great risk. Since Jesus was both a religious and a political rebel, aligning oneself to Jesus assured persecution, and many of the first Christians were brutally killed. Yet, the early Christians remained fervent in their mystical practices in their homes and other secret places. This was especially evident during the Pentecost, when the Holy Spirit overtook those present at an undisclosed location and the crowd began speaking in mysterious tongues (see Acts 2:1-4).

Between 34-37 C.E. the former Saul of Tarsus, who had persecuted the first Christians, had a mystical experience of Christ on the road to Damascus. After this experience, he converted to Christianity, changed his name to Paul, and became an apostle, spreading the Christian message throughout Asia Minor and Europe. Paul's testimony was especially powerful, for it revealed that Christ could awaken the heart at random without requiring a human intermediary or

> Theologians may quarrel, but the mystics of the world speak the same language.
>
> MEISTER ECKHART

adhering to certain doctrines. This gave Paul the green light to minister to the Gentiles, or non-Jews. This caused a great rift between him and Jesus' original disciples who focused their ministry on the Jewish population. While Jews were reluctant to become Christians, Gentiles converted by the masses, making Paul the most influential of all Christian apostles. As he traveled around he established churches in various cities, and he would occasionally write letters to guide these churches in Christian practice. These letters, the Pauline epistles, eventually became a large part of the New Testament canon.

In the following three centuries Christianity spread despite persecution. In 313 C.E., Christianity was finally legalized. Nearly seventy years later (380 C.E.), Christianity was made the official religion of the Roman Empire under Emperor Theodosius I. As politics became intermingled with Christian spiritual practice, doctrines soon dominated the Christian experience. Rome led the charge in the establishment of these doctrines, with their primary aim being to create order amongst diverse Christian groups that were often bickering. Those authorized doctrines soon replaced individual mystical experience as the pathway to God, and any experience that strayed away from these authorized doctrines bordered on heresy. Access to God was placed in the hands of the Church.

Christian mysticism still endured through certain individuals. In the third century, some Christians sold all their possessions and headed for the Sahara desert in order to connect with God while limiting worldly distractions. These individuals became known as the Desert Fathers and Mothers. It was through the Desert Fathers and Mothers that Christian mysticism was rediscovered and popularized. Notable Desert Fathers and Mothers included Paul of Thebes, Anthony the Great, Arsenius the Great, Poemen, Macarius of Egypt, Moses the Black, Syncletica of Alexandria, Pachomius, Shenouda the Archimandrite, Athanasius of Alexandria, John Chrysostom, Evagrius Ponticus,

Hilarion, John Cassian, Amma Syncletica of Alexandria, Theodora of Alexandria, Amma Sarah of the Desert, Melania the Elder, Melania the Younger, Olympias, Saint Paula, and Eustochium.

In the centuries that followed, Rome fell and split into two smaller kingdoms: the Western Roman Empire, centered on Latin-speaking Rome, and the Eastern Roman Empire (Byzantine), centered on Greek-speaking Constantinople. Very quickly mysticism found its way into the religious practices of the Eastern Roman Empire. With an emphasis on contemplative prayer and the mystery of God, the Eastern Christians connected with God by concentrating the mind on God's eternal presence and repeating the Jesus Prayer ("Lord Jesus Christ, Son of God, have mercy on me, a sinner."). This became known as Hesychasm. In later centuries, Christian mystics such as Symeon the New Theologian and Gregory Palamas further developed the Hesychast tradition, and Hesychasm eventually made its way into the Slavic lands and Russia, where works such as the *Philokalia* were produced.

In the Western Roman Empire, Christian mysticism was also practiced but to a lesser extent. It wasn't until the 9th century when Johannes Scotus Erigena, who knew Greek, translated the writings of several of the Eastern Christian mystics and introduced his translations to the West. Monasticism soon became a popular spiritual pathway in the West, giving individuals who chose such a path the opportunity to delve into the interior world of mysticism. Notable Christian mystics in the following centuries included Bernard of Clarvaux, Richard of Saint-Victor, Hildegard of Bingen, Elizabeth of Schonau, St. Francis of Assisi, Bonaventure, Meister Eckhart, Hadewijch of Brabant, Mechthild von Magdeburg, Marguerite Porete, Clare of Assisi, Angela da

> The Christian of the future will be a mystic or he will not exist at all.
>
> **KARL RAHNER**

Foligno, Henrich Suso, Johann Tauler, Jan van Ruysbroeck, Catherine of Siena, Catherine of Genoa, Richard Rolle, Joan of Arc, Walter Hilton, Julian of Norwich, and the author of *The Cloud of Unknowing*.

When the Protestant Reformation unfolded in the West in the 16th century, mysticism was widely abandoned for a more rational, biblically-centered Christian experience. Nevertheless, within certain Catholic and Protestant communities mysticism survived. In the 16th and 17th centuries, Spanish and French mystics carried on the mystical tradition. Spanish mystics included Francis de Osuna, Luis de Leon, Luis de Grenada, Ignatius of Loyola, Teresa of Avila, and John of the Cross. French mystics included Francis of Sales, Pierre de Berulle, Brother Lawrence, and Marie Guyard. Other mystics around that time included Sebastian Franck, Valentin Weigel, Jakob Bohme, Johann Arndt, William Law, and George Fox. In the 20th century, mysticism gained popularity amongst Protestants through the works of Evelyn Underhill and Thomas Merton.

Today, Christian mysticism is seeing a new revival in the West. Spiritual seekers are beginning to favor real encounters with God rather than simply relying on doctrines about God. Nevertheless, religion still dominates much of Western Christianity with the majority of Christians following one of two major Christian pathways. In the next section, we will take a look at these two major pathways, and in the subsequent section I will talk about the third pathway of Christian mysticism that is beginning to influence Western spirituality.

The Spiritual Limitations of the Two Common Western Christian Religions

Growing up in the church, I was told that there were three practices to grow one's relationship with God: go to church, read the Bible, and pray. One may think of these three practices as the three wheels of a tricycle that is on the pathway to God. The wheel of the church allows the Christian to assemble with a group of likeminded spiritual seekers, encouraging and growing one another in Christlikeness. As Jesus said, "For when two or three are gathered together in my name, there am I in the midst of them," (Matthew 18:20). The wheel of the Bible equips the Christian with timeless spiritual truths that ground them through life's ups and downs. The wheel of prayer allows the Christian to connect with God no matter where they are or what they are doing. All three wheels are essential in growing one's relationship with God.

Of course, one wheel must lead. The front wheel is the largest of all three wheels and steers the direction of the entire tricycle. Unfortunately, the two largest Western Christian religions, Catholicism and Protestantism, choose to lead with the wrong wheel forward. Catholics lead by the wheel of the church, what they consider to be the mediary between man and God. Protestants, on the other hand, lead by the wheel of the Bible, which they likewise see as the ultimate mediary between man and God. As a result, both Catholics and Protestants tend to rely on external sources about God apart from a personal and direct relationship with God. To give an example: I can have a good relationship with a person's parents, siblings, and friends and have little to no relationship with that person. Similarly, I can read about that person on Facebook or Instagram and get to know them through the eyes of social media. However, it does not mean I have a strong relationship with that person. The same is true with our relationship with God. We can go to church and read the Bible all we want to; it does not mean we have a relationship with God. Let's take a look at how both the Catholic and Protestant reliances on mediaries limit deeper Christian spiritually.

Catholics depend heavily on the Church. To the Catholic, the Church is the representation of God on earth. If one wants to have a relationship with God, one has to become a member of the Church. If one sins and wants to be forgiven by God, one goes to the Church and confesses their sin to a priest, who then mediates between the confessor and God.

A fear of many Catholics is being excommunicated from the Church, for if you are excommunicated from the Church, you are excommunicated from God. Today, the Catholic Church is the largest Christian church on the planet with over 1.3 billion adherents.

Protestants are Christians who *protest* the divine authority of the Catholic Church. With the combination of the Protestant Reformation, Martin Luther's translation of the Latin Bible, and Johannes Guttenberg's invention of the printing press, Protestant communities exploded on the religious scene in the 16th century and have grown in number ever since. Today, there are nearly one billion Protestants worldwide.

Protestants hold a strong reverence towards the Bible. If you grew up in America as a Protestant, it is likely you were raised to believe that the Bible is the lone Word of God (more on this in chapter 9). The Bible, being a complex combination of books written over thousands of years, can be interpreted in a multitude of ways, depending on the reader. Consequently, hundreds of different Protestant denominations have appeared, each with their own doctrines based on their particular interpretations of the Bible. This puts many denominations at odds with one another, despite the fact that they both revere the same book. Interestingly, the book that has healed countless individuals and brought people closer to God is the same book that has been used to promote hatred, homophobia, patriarchy, slavery, and genocide.

Both Catholics and Protestants can agree that neither the Church nor the Bible *are* God, yet both Catholics and Protestants have elevated the Church and the Bible to Godlike status. I want to be very clear: this is idolatry. The Church is not God, and neither is the Bible. Viewing either as the primary source of God's revelation not only deceives the Christian to conform to manmade perspectives, but it limits their access to the God they are worshiping. In addition, being a church-going Catholic or a Bible-reading Protestant does not guarantee you have a relationship with God. You can go to church every Sunday, confess your sins, and hear empowering messages and still have a severed line to God. You can read and quote the Bible and know Hebrew and Greek and still have no communication with the Divine. What a travesty it is to remain in this state of disconnection! Perhaps we are placing the wrong foot forward. Perhaps we must surpass any human-created intermediary and go directly to the Source itself. We need to be leading by prayer.

Leading by the Third Wheel of Prayer: The Path of Christian Mysticism

I grew up in a family of prayer warriors. These prayer warriors were dedicated churchgoers and Bible readers. What distinguished them from most other Christians, however, was their prayer life. They were constantly praying, constantly communicating with God. It did not matter if they were at church or had a Bible in hand. It did not matter if they were weeding the garden or milking the cows. It did not matter if they were hanging out with outsiders or non-Christians. It didn't matter if they were hiking in the forest or involved in a team sport. It did not matter if they were adopting Eastern practices of meditation and yoga. It did not even matter if they were going through immense suffering. What mattered most was their connection to God's presence at all times, and they were intentional about bridging themselves with that presence. It was through their connection to God that miracles manifested and lives were transformed. They did all this with the wheel of prayer guiding their path forward. As the Apostle Paul instructed the Christians in Thessalonica:

> *Rejoice always, pray without ceasing, give thanks in all circumstances; for this is the will of God in Christ Jesus for you. (1 Thessalonians 5:16-18)*

While Catholics favor the Church and Protestants favor the Bible, the Christian mystic favors ceaseless prayer. Mystics may still respect the church and/or the Bible, however, prayer dominates the mystic's life. Mystics believe that God can speak to and through them, heal them, transform them, use them, and lead them. They aim to be a vessel of God's love and light, and this is only done through the opening of the self to God's presence. The mystic values their connection with God so much that they are willing to sacrifice their own religion for the sake of building this human-divine relationship.

The Mystic Shift

The shift from religion to relationship is what I call *the mystic shift*. I am writing this book, because through undergoing *the mystic shift* myself I have experienced profound spiritual breakthroughs. *The mystic shift* has liberated me from the confines of fear and anxiety, replaced instead by love, joy, and peace. *The mystic shift* has allowed me to shed layer after layer of religious dogma which kept me bound to legalism and separated me from my neighbor. *The Mystic Shift* has allowed me to stand apart from my ego that once controlled me and disabled me from love. Most of all, *The Mystic Shift* has led me to have a deeper and more meaningful relationship with God, who is now much greater than I originally perceived when I was a religious Christian. I can now sense God's presence with me in every moment.

This book is written to those Christians who are passionate about developing their relationship with God but are tired of religion. This book is written for those who have an interest in Jesus but are tired of churchy clichés that are hollow. This book is written to those who want a real, transformative relationship with God that does not require doctrinal position. To you I write this book. I want you to know you're not alone. It is likely that if you are reading this book you are a Christian who has been on a similar journey of discovering God. I hope this book encourages you to continue your spiritual journey forward, despite the persecution you might receive in your own religious community. Trust God, and lean not on your own understanding (Proverbs 3:5).

> The Christian mystic therefore is one for whom God and Christ are not merely objects of belief, but living facts experimentally known first hand.
>
> CARL McCOLMAN

In this book, I will present ten mindset shifts that are aimed to support you as you move beyond religion and develop your relationship with God. These mindset shifts have resulted in the manifestation of the fruits of the Spirit in my own life. They have enabled me to dwell in a constant state of joy and peace no matter the changing circumstances around me. It has grown my understanding of God, and my relationship with God is deeper than it has ever been before. I have gained a greater appreciation for Christianity, not as a religion but as a way of life. Jesus' teachings make sense to me, and they are extremely practical. I am also more aware of my ego. I realize it is not who I am but rather a vessel of God's love and light.

Heed my warning, though: the ten mindset shifts presented in this book may challenge your Christian perspective. The mindset shifts were written to provoke your egoic response. The internal struggle it may cause must occur if you wish to move beyond religion and into a relationship-driven life. Wrestle with each mindset shift as it is presented, and witness your own reaction. Observe your inner mental and emotional dialogue. Observe the defense mechanisms of your ego fighting to stay relevant. By observing your mental and emotional reactions you will create the space necessary to move beyond them. Your level of self-awareness will subsequently grow as you better identify your reactions when they take place.

When I am presented with new and possibly contradictory

information, I like to do a quick mental practice that helps open up my mind (I learned this practice from spiritual author and teacher Gregg Braden). Imagine taking your established beliefs and putting them in a mental file folder labeled "My Beliefs." Next, imagine taking this file folder and placing it in the back of your mind to be stored safely and retrieved at a later time. Then, imagine opening a new file folder labeled "Possibilities." As you are presented with new information, imagine placing this information into the new file folder. Upon conclusion of each chapter, you may decide to keep the new file folder open permanently to contemplate, or perhaps you will decide to bring your old file folder back into the forefront of your mind. The choice is ultimately yours. I encourage you to try this mental practice out.

The following are the ten mindset shifts presented in this book:

From Sinner to Vessel: How We View Ourselves

From Judgment to Love: How We View Others

From Concept to Mystery: How We View God

From Belief to Liberation: How We View Salvation

From Disobedience to Opportunity: How We View Sin

From Fear to Faith: How We View the Unknown

From Paradise to Presence: How We View Heaven and Earth

From Closed Book to Open Revelation: How We View God's Word

From Building to Assembly: How We View the Church

From Conversion to Awakening: How We View the Great Commission

At the end of each chapter are reflection questions designed to assist you in your inner journey. I have also included a prayer practice that when implemented will help you deepen the human-divine connection. I highly recommend keeping a journal for your self-reflections and prayer practices as you track your spiritual growth.

The mystic shift may revolutionize your life. You may lose all desire to return to your former beliefs, for you will see the illusions of religion which once kept you bound. As you wrestle with this inner transformation, you will wrestle with your foundational beliefs. You will be led into the dark night of your soul where religion simply cannot survive. You will fight to exit this place. You will desperately hold onto your old identity as it suffers and dies. It is difficult to know how long you will be in this dark night, but eventually you will see the light of God shine through when you fully surrender yourself to the transformation of the Spirit. What comes after is a glorious resurrection, initiated by God who will then restore your spirit, build your vessel, guide you into the future, and love you in your entirety. I pray that God opens your heart and mind and enriches you as you traverse through the wilderness of your endless soul.

May God guide you on this journey.

Amen.

Reflection Questions

1. What doctrines am I currently attached to?

   _____

   _____

   _____

   _____

2. How would my life change if I focused on building my prayer life?

   _____

   _____

   _____

   _____

3. What is holding me back from fully giving myself to God?

   _____

   _____

   _____

Prayer Practice

In order to hear from God, one must make time for God daily. This is the first step towards *The Mystic Shift*. Making time to consistently connect with God will bring about its challenges. You may lack motivation. Connect with God anyway. You may get distracted and miss a day. Start again the next day without self-judgment. For a new behavior to become a habit, it will require consistent practice for at least two months.

If you already have a meditation, contemplation, or prayer practice, great! If you do not, I suggest turning on some soft instrumental or meditation music. There are numerous guided meditations you can try online as well. Your goal right now is to just find the time every day to meditate/contemplate/pray. Twenty or thirty minutes should suffice. I highly recommend journaling after every experience.

1

From Sinner to Vessel:

How We View Ourselves

I WANT YOU TO KNOW SOMETHING, my friend: God loves you.

God loves you exactly as you are. You do not need to change anything about yourself for God to love you. No matter your current struggles; no matter your glaring weaknesses; no matter your sin or imperfection, you are fully loved by God. In fact, God loves you so much that God created you in God's very image.

So God created man in his own image, in the image of God he created him; male and female he created them. (Genesis 1:27)

You are an expression of God, a vessel of God's very light. Just as light has various wavelengths which result in a wide variety of colors, God, as the light, is expressed uniquely in every human being.

You, as God's unique expression, are extremely beautiful. There is no other expression like you! Indeed, as God's expression you are very good.

God saw all that he had made, and it was very good. (Genesis 1:31)

Yet, for many of us, we were raised to believe that we are bad. We were taught early on that our human nature is evil. We maintain the view that we are wretched sinners that God is extremely displeased with. We believe we must earn God's love, that we must change. It is difficult for us to see God's love as unconditional.

So which is it: are we good or are we bad? Are we loved by God or rejected by God? Let us take a look at the story that is often used to evaluate these questions.

> *Now the serpent was more crafty than any of the wild animals the Lord God had made. He said to the woman, "Did God really say, 'You must not eat from any tree in the garden'?"*
>
> *The woman said to the serpent, "We may eat fruit from the trees in the garden, but God did say, 'You must not eat fruit from the tree that is in the middle of the garden, and you must not touch it, or you will die.'"*
>
> *"You will not certainly die," the serpent said to the woman. "For God knows that when you eat from it your eyes will be opened, and you will be like God, knowing good and evil."*
>
> *When the woman saw that the fruit of the tree was good for food and pleasing to the eye, and also desirable for gaining wisdom, she took some and ate it. She also gave some to her husband, who was with her, and he ate it. Then the eyes of both of them were opened, and they realized they were naked; so they sewed fig leaves together and made coverings for themselves.*
>
> *Then the man and his wife heard the sound of the Lord God as he was walking in the garden in the cool of the day, and they hid from the Lord God among the trees of the garden. But the Lord God called to the man, "Where are you?"*
>
> *He answered, "I heard you in the garden, and I was afraid because I was naked; so I hid."*
>
> *And he said, "Who told you that you were naked? Have you eaten from the tree that I commanded you not to eat from?"*
>
> *The man said, "The woman you put here with me—she gave me some fruit from the tree, and I ate it."*
>
> *Then the Lord God said to the woman, "What is this you have done?"*

The woman said, "The serpent deceived me, and I ate."

So the Lord God said to the serpent, "Because you have done this,

"Cursed are you above all livestock

and all wild animals!

You will crawl on your belly

and you will eat dust

all the days of your life.

And I will put enmity

between you and the woman,

and between your offspring and hers;

he will crush your head,

and you will strike his heel."

To the woman he said,

"I will make your pains in childbearing very severe;

with painful labor you will give birth to children.

Your desire will be for your husband, and he will rule over you."

To Adam he said, "Because you listened to your wife and ate fruit from the tree about which I commanded you, 'You must not eat from it,'

"Cursed is the ground because of you;

through painful toil you will eat food from it

all the days of your life.

It will produce thorns and thistles for you,

and you will eat the plants of the field.

By the sweat of your brow

you will eat your food

until you return to the ground,

since from it you were taken;

for dust you are and to dust you will return."

Adam named his wife Eve, because she would become the mother

> To be yourself in a world that is constantly trying to make you something else is the greatest accomplishment.
>
> **RALPH W. EMERSON**

> Respect your uniqueness.
> Drop comparison.
> Relax into your being.
>
> RUMI

of all the living.

The Lord God made garments of skin for Adam and his wife and clothed them. And the Lord God said, "The man has now become like one of us, knowing good and evil. He must not be allowed to reach out his hand and take also from the tree of life and eat, and live forever." So the Lord God banished him from the Garden of Eden to work the ground from which he had been taken. After he drove the man out, he placed on the east side of the Garden of Eden cherubim and a flaming sword flashing back and forth to guard the way to the tree of life. (Genesis 3)

According to mainstream Christian doctrine, Adam and Eve's fall brought sin into the world, creating a barrier between man and God. Some Christians even claim that Adam and Eve's fall led to all humans inheriting a sinful nature at birth. Even an adorable newborn baby is a wretched sinner. Only if one converts to Christianity can one overcome their fallen nature and be reunified with God and escape eternal torment.

What a sad and punitive view of our blessed humanity, and what a sad misrepresentation of God.

When reading the story of the fall of Adam and Eve, one is not immediately led to the conclusion that all humans are rotten sinners. In

> Today you are you, that is truer than true. There is no one alive who is youer than you.
>
> DR. SEUSS

fact, the doctrine of original sin was developed much later. So if the story of Adam and Eve's fall is not about how humans became sinners, what is the story about? The key to that question lies in the serpent. The serpent was the craftiest of all the animals God created. The serpent was a trickster, a deceiver who tempted Adam and Eve. Centuries later the serpent gained the reputation as the devil. The serpent is, in fact, a symbol of a much greater spiritual adversary. Before we look at this adversary, I think it would be beneficial to reflect on our own prehistory.

From Hunter-Gatherers to Civilization

For ninety percent of our human history, we were hunter-gatherers. We were nomadic, wandering from place to place following herds of large animals that we hunted for food. Plants and other wild edibles were gathered as well. Every time we killed an animal or gathered a plant, we would thank the animal or plant and utilize every part of it. Truly, we were connected to the earth. We were animistic, believing every animal or plant had a spirit. We respected all life, for we believed the spirit was within all life. We organized ourselves into small groups or tribes. Life was built on trust, and we shared our limited resources with one another. There were certainly disputes, but they were settled quickly, for there was no need for additional burdens. Every member in the tribe shared an equal responsibility of caring for one another. There was no king or queen. There was no upper class or lower class. Every individual was the tribe.

Then everything changed with the planting of a single seed. We went from living a nomadic lifestyle to living in permanent settlements, surviving off the abundance of crops we learned to grow and the animals we domesticated. Some of us were quick to make land and animal claims, accumulating great wealth and power

> You are unrepeatable. There is a magic about you that is all your own.
>
> D.M. DELLINGER

> Always remember that
> you are absolutely unique.
> Just like everyone else.
>
> MARGARET MEAD

in the process. Most of us, however, were forced to rely on the landowning elites for survival. Inequality became the new normal. As populations grew, cities were erected, and with them came the rise of governments and religions, administered by the landowning elites, who were most often men. As more cities were established and grew in size, conflicts between various cities became frequent. This oftentimes escalated in warfare, as kingdoms sought to expand and control more lands. The results of war were genocide, slavery, and oppression. Disease also spread, especially amongst city-dwellers, who came in close contact with domesticated animals.

The Agricultural Revolution changed everything. While our hunter-gatherer ancestors struggled for survival, they trusted one another and trusted that the earth would provide. When civilization arose, our ancestors soon replaced this trust with fear. The earth went from being a place that provided to a place that had to be overcome. People went from perceived helpers to perceived threats. As this fear of the outside intensified, our ancestors created barriers between themselves and the rest of the earth.

Perhaps the story of Adam and Eve's fall from the Garden of Eden tells the story of our transition from the hunting-gathering lifestyle to civilization. Adam and Eve wanted to be like God, and thus replaced God with their own human drives. As a result, they fell into destruction. Similarly, as we transitioned to civilization we lost our spiritual nature of trust and connection with all and became possessed by fear and the desire to separate from others, from the earth, and from God. We ultimately lost faith that God would provide, and instead put our faith in a force that has been ruling human consciousness ever since: the Great Egoic Consciousness.

The Rise of the Great Egoic Consciousness

It has been called the Tempter. It has been called the Adversary. It is what Christians call the Devil, Satan, or Lucifer. It has been referred to as "the ways of the world." Chinese folk religions call it the Demonic Influence. In Confucianism, it correlates with wrong behavior. In Taoism, it is what brings an individual away from the virtues of compassion, moderation, and humility. Friedrich Nietzsche named it the functional non-good. The Egyptians knew it as Isfet or disorder. Buddhists call it suffering. Hindus see it as bad action. Whatever name it is given, it is the same collective force across all cultures. I will call it the Great Egoic Consciousness.

> Through pride we are ever deceiving ourselves. But deep down below the surface of the average conscience a still, small voice says to us, something is out of tune.
>
> C.G. JUNG

There is a reason I call this force the *Great Egoic Consciousness*. It is *Great* because it is bigger than any one individual, and no one individual has control over it. It is *Egoic* because it operates through the ego, both individual and collective, distracting the soul from seeing their true spiritual nature. It is *Consciousness* because it is dynamic and dwells primarily in the human mind.

The Great Egoic Consciousness is not a person, though in many religious traditions it has been personified. It is a force that actively distracts, takes, steals, tempts, and destroys. It holds its victims firmly in its grasp and blinds the individual from seeing beyond it. It has snuck into our society and our institutions, notably politics, economics, and religion. It influences the media and daily conversations. Most of us are unaware of its presence, for it is a trickster, deceiving us into believing it gives life and is our identity.

The Great Egoic Consciousness thrives off of fear and separation.

> Pride must die in you,
> or nothing of heaven
> can live in you.
>
> ANDREW MURRAY

It brews within the individual a general distrust towards others and a general distrust towards the earth. It encourages the individual to put trust only in themselves, eliminating any real need for faith in others or in God. It manipulates the individual to see themselves as separate from and holier than others.

Jesus himself was tempted by the Great Egoic Consciousness. It is what Luke refers to as the devil.

> *Jesus, full of the Holy Spirit, left the Jordan and was led by the Spirit into the wilderness, where for forty days he was tempted by the devil. He ate nothing during those days, and at the end of them he was hungry.*
>
> *The devil said to him, "If you are the Son of God, tell this stone to become bread."*
>
> *Jesus answered, "It is written: 'Man shall not live on bread alone.'"*
>
> *The devil led him up to a high place and showed him in an instant all the kingdoms of the world. And he said to him, "I will give you all their authority and splendor; it has been given to me, and I can give it to anyone I want to. If you worship me, it will all be yours."*
>
> *Jesus answered, "It is written: 'Worship the Lord your God and serve him only.'"*
>
> *The devil led him to Jerusalem and had him stand on the highest point of the temple. "If you are the Son of God," he said, "throw yourself down from here. For it is written:*
>
> *"He will command his angels concerning you*
> *to guard you carefully;*
> *they will lift you up in their hands,*
> *so that you will not strike your foot against a stone.'"*
>
> *Jesus answered, "It is said: 'Do not put the Lord your God to the test.'"*

When the devil had finished all this tempting, he left him until an opportune time. (Luke 4:1-13)

Being a deceiver, the Great Egoic Consciousness is difficult to recognize. Though we are often unaware of its presence, there is a feature it displays that makes it possible to identify. That feature is pride.

Pride costs us more than hunger, thirst, and cold.

THOMAS JEFFERSON

Pride: The Drive to Separate and Elevate Oneself

Pride, also called vanity, is an emotional response that aims to elevate one's self-worth above that of everybody else. C.S. Lewis gives a great description of pride in his book *Mere Christianity*:

> *The vice I am talking of is Pride or Self-Conceit: and the virtue opposite to it, in Christian morals, is called Humility...According to Christian teachers, the essential vice, the utmost evil, is Pride. Unchastity, anger, greed, drunkenness, and all that, are mere flea bites in comparison: it was through Pride that the devil became the devil: Pride leads to every other vice: it is the complete anti-God state of mind.*

Lewis continues:

> *Pride gets no pleasure out of having something, only out of having more of it than the next man. We say that people are proud of being rich, or clever, or good-looking, but they are not. They are proud of being richer, cleverer, or better-looking than others. If everyone else became equally rich, or clever, or good-looking there would be nothing to be proud about. It is the comparison that makes you proud: the pleasure of being above the rest. Once the element of competition has gone, pride has gone.*

Since the rise of civilization, pride has been fashioned as a virtue. This is especially true in American society, which bases their entire economic system on competition. To have success in American society, one must compete and ultimately conquer their competitors. It is no wonder America is full of prideful people. Pride is taught and encouraged from a very early age. Americans have pride in their nation. Americans have pride in their sports teams. Americans have pride in their political affiliation. Americans have pride in their education. Americans have pride in their accomplishments. Americans have pride in their religion. Pride drives the American to separate from all things and elevate themselves on an imaginary pedestal.

Pride carries over to Christianity as well. In Christianity, pride is veiled behind the Christian image. It is taught that Christianity is the only pathway to God, and one ought to be proud of their Christian identity.

To many Christians, God is believed to have human emotions. God is jealous of our attention, and God gets angry when we don't give him that attention. God is like a second grader who has trouble controlling his emotions and is very quick to react. Many Christians believe that God demands perfection, and those that fail to meet this perfection will face his eternal wrath. As all of us fail to meet God's expectations, either we burn in hell or a sacrifice must be made to God. This is where Jesus is most often placed in Christian theology, as a blood sacrifice to an angry God who is extremely disappointed in our shortcomings.

> **I am God's creation, designed according to His plan for me.**
>
> NICK VUJICIC

Yet, if God is love and created humanity in his own image, how can God ever reject us? How likely is it for a father to reject his son or daughter, even if they did wicked things? Are human fathers more loving than God? It does not make sense. Did Jesus really come as an atoning sacrifice to appease a pissed-off God, or did Jesus come to revolutionize the way *we* understand God? Thirteenth century Scottish priest John Duns Scotus gave an amazing statement that I believe every Christian needs to reflect upon:

> *Jesus didn't come into the world to change God's mind about us; God so loves the world. Jesus came to change the mind of humanity about God.*

God's mind does not need changing. God is perfect in essence and love, the same yesterday, today, and forever. God is not bound to fickle human emotions as many Christians perceive. It is us who are bound. It is us who are imperfect. It is our minds that need changing. Perhaps the greatest change we need to make as Christians is how we understand ourselves. Perhaps the most destructive theology within Christianity is the theology that teaches that all humans are sinners, suggesting that "sinner" is our very identity. What hogwash! Sin is an action, not a noun (more on sin in Chapter 5). To undergo *the mystic shift* we must first change the way we see ourselves.

You are a Unique Vessel of God

What if instead of fearing our humanity we embraced it? What if instead of expecting perfection we learned from our imperfection? What if instead of perceiving that we must do something to earn God's love that we start to see ourselves as loved by God already?

It is time to get rid of the "sinner" mindset which has kept Christians bound to fear, guilt, and shame, qualities that

> While I know myself as a creation of God, I am also obligated to realize and remember that everyone else and everything else are also God's creation.
>
> MAYA ANGELOU

resemble the Great Egoic Consciousness. It is time to re-discover our true identity as vessels of God, as spiritual beings who are having a human experience. As the 11th/12th century German mystic Hildegard of Bingen said:

> *A human being is a vessel that God has built for himself and filled with his inspiration so that his works are perfected in it.*

We are portals of God, and like Jesus, through our human vessels God is manifested on earth. Jesus did not identify humans as sinners. Jesus did not even believe in original sin! No, Jesus taught that we are the light of the world (Matthew 5:14) and that the kingdom of God is within us (Luke 17:21). No matter how much we have sinned or how broken we are, God can still shine love and light through us into this world.

You, in your true spiritual nature, are very good. You are unconditionally loved by God and will always be loved by God. You will fall short; that is what it means to be human. Yet, as a broken vessel, God will uniquely shine through you. As the Israelite prophet Isaiah said:

> *We are the clay, you are the potter; we are all the work of your hand.* (Isaiah 64:8)

Are you ready to let go of the "sinner" mentality? Are you ready to embrace who you really are, a child of God created in God's likeness? If so, I encourage you to open your vessel.

Reflection Questions

1. Where does the Great Egoic Consciousness hold the most power in my life?

   _____

   _____

   _____

2. In what areas of my life am I prideful?

   _____

   _____

   _____

3. What are my strengths, skills, talents, and interests?

   _____

   _____

   _____

4. Where do I feel called to be the greatest expression of God's love and light?

   _____

   _____

   _____

Prayer Practice

The Hebrew word *ruach* means breath, wind, and spirit. In the Hebrew language, breath and spirit are the same. God *breathed* into Adam and gave him life. At our death, we *breathe* our last breath and give up our spirit.

As you continue your prayer practice, focus on your breath. On every inhale and exhale, mentally tell yourself the following words:

I am the breath of God.

2

Judgment to Love:

How We View Others

WHEN MY GRANDPA was in his 50's he was asked to share his testimony one Sunday with a small congregation in McKenna, Washington. After he gave his testimony, the ladies aide (women who raise money for their church) asked him to be their lead pastor. At first he was reluctant, feeling unworthy of such a position as he was an eighth grade dropout and was never ordained by a church or university. However, God gave him peace of heart to take the position, telling him "I ordained you." For the next three decades, my grandpa led and grew that church.

My grandpa was a unique pastor in the community in that he cared more for people than he did religious rules. His ministry focused on restoration. He believed that no matter who the person was or what they struggled with, God loved them and longed to have a relationship with them. My grandpa had a heart for the broken, an ear for the suppressed, and a love for the sinner. When my grandpa and grandma would go to the mall, my grandpa would tell my grandma to go shopping while he sought out the loneliest person in the mall. He would go over to them, put his arm around them, and tell him or her that God loves them.

At church, my grandpa gave all people the opportunity to minister, no matter their present lifestyle. In doing this, however, the church

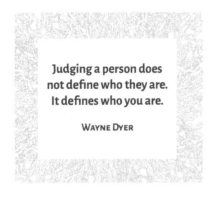

> Judging a person does not define who they are. It defines who you are.
>
> **WAYNE DYER**

board confronted him, telling him that he should never be allowing certain individuals to minister. He ignored their criticism, and several years later church board members showed up at his doorstep with a letter asking for his resignation. My grandpa accepted with a broken heart. Nevertheless, he went on to minister to whomever he encountered until his death.

The Declining Church

The church in the West is drastically declining. People inside the church reason this decline is due to the "Great Falling Away" as portrayed in end-times theology. They believe the ones leaving the church have rejected God and are at fault. When talking directly with the people who have left the church, however, a different understanding emerges. According to many who have left the church, their main reason for leaving is because church members are hypocritical and too judgmental. Perhaps the churchgoing Christian needs to take a good look in the mirror and assess whether their level of hypocrisy and judgment is driving people away. To the church going Christian, I recommend you read, reflect, and contemplate on the following teaching of Jesus.

> *Do not judge, or you too will be judged. For in the same way you judge others, you will be judged, and with the measure you use, it will be measured to you.*
>
> *Why do you look at the speck of sawdust in your brother's eye and pay no attention to the plank in your own eye? How can you say to your brother, 'Let me take the speck out of your eye,' when all the time*

there is a plank in your own eye? You hypocrite! First take the plank
out of your own eye, and then you will see clearly to remove the speck
from your brother's eye. (Matthew 7:1-5)

Not only was Jesus teaching to cease from judgment, but he subsequently called out judgmental people as hypocrites! Funny that these are the same two reasons why people say they are leaving the church today. Throughout the Gospels Jesus frequently accused the religious leaders of his day for judging the misdeeds of others. The Pharisees were especially targeted by Jesus because of their constant finger-pointing. Jesus asked any Pharisee who was without sin to step forward and cast the first stone (John 8:7). No Pharisee could step forward with integrity, knowing full well that their hypocrisy would be exposed. This angered them considerably.

The sin we all carry within us is the plank that Jesus is referring to (we will look at sin in more detail in chapter 5). As we all sin, we all have distorted perceptions due to the plank, so it makes sense why Jesus taught his followers to refrain from judgment. Let us take a closer look at the attitude of judgment.

Superiority Complex of Judgment

Judgment is the result of an individual's superiority complex. The superiority complex is an attitude of superiority that actually covers up feelings of inferiority created by failure (sin). Judging others is a reaction of this complex. People with a strong superiority complex want to portray

> Our job is to love others without stopping to inquire whether or not they are worthy.
>
> **THOMAS MERTON**

themselves as holier than the "sinners" over there. They want to paint a picture that they are more spiritual, more Christian, and/or closer to God. The superiority complex's greatest power is covering up one's own failures (from both the public eye and from one's own awareness). By hiding their own failures they cannot be viewed on equivalent grounds as those they are judging.

Today, the superiority complex is rampant in the church. We have all likely experienced it on some level. I have experienced it several times myself. I have seen my friends and family judged by Christians as less Godly. I read judgmental comments all the time on social media from churchgoing people judging the sins of others. Why are we deliberately ignoring Jesus' teaching on judgment? His instruction has obviously fallen on deaf ears.

Love as a Command

Judgment was condemned, not commanded by Jesus. Why? Because judgment is a sin, as it has the power to restrict love. As Mother Teresa said, "If you judge people, you have no time to love them." While Jesus discouraged judgment of others in all situations, he did teach the proper Christian response. When asked by his disciples, "Teacher, which is the greatest commandment in the Law?" Jesus replied with the following:

> If you judge people you have no time to love them.
>
> MOTHER TERESA

'Love the Lord your God with all your heart and with all your soul and with all your mind.' This is the first and greatest commandment. And the second is like it: 'Love your neighbor as yourself.' All the Law and the Prophets hang on these two commandments. (Matthew 22:36-40)

All the law can be summed up into one commandment: love. Whether you are loving God or you are loving others, it is the same commandment of love. If there is a practice that Christians ought to adopt, if there is any commandment they ought to center their doctrines and theology upon, it is love. If Jesus' words are not enough to convince you to love, let us take another passage of scripture. In the book of 1 John, John the Evangelist echoed the earlier words of Jesus:

> *Dear friends, let us love one another, for love comes from God.*
> *Everyone who loves has been born of God and knows God. Whoever*
> *does not love does not know God, because God is love. (1 John 4:7-8)*

John gives us the exact definition of love. *God is love.* So by loving your neighbor, you are expressing God's very essence. If love is within you, God is within you. On the other hand, if you do not love your neighbor, you don't know God. Wow! Let us take another scripture to further justify this commandment. This time we will look at the words of Paul.

> *If I speak in the tongues of men or of angels, but do not have love,*
> *I am only a resounding gong or a clanging cymbal. If I have the gift*
> *of prophecy and can fathom all mysteries and all knowledge, and if*
> *I have a faith that can move mountains, but do not have love, I am*
> *nothing. If I give all I possess to the poor and give over my body to*
> *hardship that I may boast, but do not have love, I gain nothing.*
>
> *Love is patient, love is*
> *kind. It does not envy, it does*
> *not boast, it is not proud. It*
> *does not dishonor others, it*
> *is not self-seeking, it is not*
> *easily angered, it keeps no*
> *record of wrongs. Love does*
> *not delight in evil but rejoices*

> **Love is the absence of judgment.**
>
> DALAI LAMA

with the truth. *It always protects, always trusts, always hopes, always perseveres.*

Love never fails. But where there are prophecies, they will cease; where there are tongues, they will be stilled; where there is knowledge, it will pass away. For we know in part and we prophesy in part, but when completeness comes, what is in part disappears. When I was a child, I talked like a child, I thought like a child, I reasoned like a child. When I became a man, I put the ways of childhood behind me. For now we see only a reflection as in a mirror; then we shall see face to face. Now I know in part; then I shall know fully, even as I am fully known.

And now these three remain: faith, hope and love. But the greatest of these is love. (1 Corinthians 13)

Love is the ultimate Christian action. Love is greater than knowing the scriptures. Love is greater than prophesying or speaking in tongues. Love is even greater than faith, which many Christians claim is the ultimate act of a Christian. If three various New Testament authors are not enough to convince you of the call to love, let us take one more verse, this time going back to the words of Jesus as told in the Gospel of John.

A new commandment I give you: love one another. As I have loved you, so you also must love one another. By this everyone will know that you are my disciples, if you love one another. (John 13:34-35)

The true witness of Jesus is not somebody who shouts on the rooftops, "I am a Christian!" or "I love Jesus!" Nobody cares what you claim to be; they care how you treat them. The true witness of Jesus is someone who loves others unconditionally, no matter their lifestyle or beliefs. This is how others will know

> We do not judge the people we love.
>
> JEAN PAUL SARTE

you are a disciple of Jesus. Jesus was the ultimate lover. He loved the outcasts. He was there for the broken. He ate with sinners. He hung out with prostitutes. He welcomed the Samaritans. Jesus loved those that society and his own religion presumed unworthy.

Loving your neighbor is not an easy task, but it is foundational if we claim to be followers of Jesus. Unfortunately, the world does not see Christians in that light. We have generally done a poor job at living the words of Jesus. Nevertheless, I believe we have a grand opportunity to change this perception moving forward, and we can do this by the very act of love itself. Love isn't just a random Christian action; love *is* the way of Christ.

Four Love Tips

Below is a strategy I have found extremely helpful in building strong and healthy relationships with a wide array of people. Implement them into your life and watch love become your primary language.

Step 1: Listen. Become an intentional listener. Be fully present to the person who is sharing. You are not just hearing them talk, waiting to give your two-cents. You are actively listening to what the person is saying. You have two ears and one mouth for a reason. Listen twice as often as you speak.

Step 2: Understand. Swiss mystic Adrienne von Speyr once said, "The first step in learning to love others is the attempt to understand them." The whole point of listening to another is to understand what the person is trying to communicate to you. Ask questions for clarity. Repeat main points back and wait to be corrected of any misunderstanding (notice they are correcting you, you are not correcting them!).

Step 3: Accept. You heard and understood their story. Now accept their story as it is and have compassion. No matter how much you may disagree with their choices or want to give your advice, keep your judgments to yourself. Remember that you are not the expert of their story. Accept the person's struggle without trying to solve the struggle for them.

Step 4: Share. If the opportunity allows, share your own story. Share how you dealt with your own struggles and what strategies you found effective. Your story may not make a difference, and that is okay. Just your presence and care alone may have planted a seed of transformation. They may decide to follow a different path than you took. Accept that. Do not try to convert them or tell them your way is best.

> In the end, nothing we do or say in this lifetime will matter as much as the way we have loved one another.
>
> DAPHNE ROSE KINGMA

You always have a choice to either judge people or to love them. Err on the side of love. When you consciously shift from judging others to loving others, your influence will grow, your relationships will prosper, and your connection with God will deepen. I encourage you to make the conscious decision to love. Christian mystic Thomas Merton summarizes it well:

Our job is to love others without stopping to inquire whether or not they are worthy. That is not our business and, in fact, it is nobody's business. What we are asked to do is to love, and this love itself will render both ourselves and our neighbors worthy.

Reflection Questions

1. What lifestyles do I find difficult to accept in other people?

   _____

   _____

   _____

2. What plank(s) do I carry?

   _____

   _____

   _____

3. How can I better love others?

   _____

   _____

   _____

4. What would a love-driven community look like?

   _____

   _____

   _____

Prayer   Practice

Think about people in your life that you are currently judging. Write their names down and the reason you are judging them. Then go into your prayer practice.

While in prayer, bring up the various reasons you are judging others, one at a time. Make it an intention to separate and create space from your thoughts. Observe each thought as it comes into your mind. After you get a good idea how your mind dialogues, bring your focus to your emotions. How are these judgments making you feel? What are your emotions telling you? Do this process with each critique and observe your reactions.

Next, picture each person you are judging in your mind's eye. As you inhale, visualize God's love entering your whole body, mind, and soul. As you exhale, send this love to the person you are picturing and say, "I send you love." Do this for seven inhales and seven exhales for each person.

3

From Concept to Mystery:

How We View God

WHEN I WAS IN COLLEGE I fell in love with learning. I loved growing my mind. I became an educator, because I wanted to expand the minds of my pupils so that they too would experience the same grandeur in learning I had experienced.

After I graduated from college I had further academic aspirations. I intended to get my Master's Degree and later my Ph.D. I believed by doing this I would be more respected in my chosen field. I also believed rigorous intellectual study would deepen my relationship with God. As I continued to learn more, however, I realized my relationship with God was not growing. I studied Christian theology, Christian history, and the Bible, yet I felt I had stalled in my relationship with God. How was it that I could study all the things about God and remain stationary in my relationship with God? I began to question whether God could even be understood. I was desperate to know God at a much deeper level. I came to realize that the accumulation of knowledge is *not* the access point to the Divine.

The Mind: The Idol of the Western World

Seventeenth century French philosopher René Descartes, widely regarded as the father of modern philosophy, once famously said, "I think, therefore I am." This proclamation introduced left-brain rationalism. Rationalism was a much-needed development in the West and is often credited for helping us emerge out of the Dark Ages, which were dominated by absolute monarchs and the fixed dogmas of the church. Through rationalism, an individual could reason for themselves what truth is instead of blindly trusting political and church authorities to dictate truth to them. This intellectual revolution opened the door to new political, economic, and religious understandings.

The mind became the official "god" of the Western world. The focus on the intellect still dominates Western society today. The educational system is a prime example of this, as it places the greatest value on the left-brain functions of language development and mathematics. Students are taught from a very young age that success is determined by high academic achievement and outperforming others. College is the ultimate goal the educational system emphasizes. College is not a horrible goal, as there are huge advantages in getting a college degree. When one experiences life beyond college, however, one may soon discover that success in school doesn't always translate to success in life. I discovered this myself. I had successfully completed 4 ½ years of vigorous undergraduate study and graduated with a degree in Social Science Education. Nevertheless, I struggled to land a job and pay my bills. I struggled in my relationships and with emotional regulation. I was not happy, and I did not experience the success I thought I would.

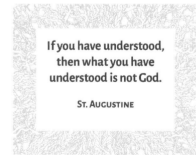

If you have understood, then what you have understood is not God.

St. Augustine

Several months before I graduated from college I fell into a major depression. Joy was vanquished. Peace became an impossibility. My mind constantly repeated negative thoughts, which brought me to extreme emotional lows. For four months I experienced hell.

The fullness of joy is to behold God in everything.

JULIAN OF NORWICH

One day I came across Eckhart Tolle's book *The Power of Now*. Reading that he suffered from depression himself, I was quick to order a copy. As soon as I received the book in the mail, I read it from cover to cover in a few days (it usually takes me months to read a book!). After reading the book I had come to learn something about myself that totally changed the way I saw the spiritual world: *I am not my mind*. Tolle explained:

> *The philosopher Descartes believed he had found the most fundamental truth when he made his famous statement, "I think, therefore I am." He had, in fact, given expression to the most basic error: to equate thinking with being and identify with thinking.*

Growing up I believed my mind and my spirit were synonymous. I believed that our bodies would someday perish, but our minds and the memories they carried would live on forever with my spirit in heaven. This was comforting to me. I cherished the memories I had and the knowledge I had gained in this life and never wanted to lose them. Then in the early 2000s my grandma was diagnosed with dementia. Over a period of five years I watched as her mind was eaten away. The vast number of memories she once vocalized dwindled to a few. It was absolutely heartbreaking for all of us to watch. But as my grandmother lost her memory something else stood out to me: her spirit was more radiant than ever. I then came to realize Eckhart Tolle was right: we are not

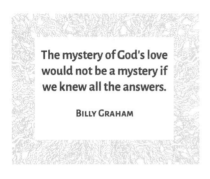

The mystery of God's love would not be a mystery if we knew all the answers.

BILLY GRAHAM

our minds, which will die along with our bodies. Rather, beneath both our minds and bodies is the eternal spirit, a consciousness that has been here long before the creation of our present life. This same spirit arises from and returns to God at our death.

The spirit is *not* synonymous with the mind. Our mind is merely an attribute of this temporary human vessel, along with our body and our emotions. All three attributes play host to our eternal spirit: our mind channels the consciousness that we are; our bodies sense the external world in which we explore; our emotions let us feel the depths of the human experience. All three attributes (mind, body, emotions) form our unique human makeup, our spirit vehicle, or what I like to call our vessel of God.

While thoughts, feelings, and sensations are necessary to being human, attachment to any of these attributes robs our soul from seeing its true essence as a voice of God. Perhaps a rephrasing of Descartes famous saying is necessary:

I am; therefore I think.

An Attempt to Describe a Mysterious God

If our minds and our spirits are not aligned, then neither are our concepts about God aligned with the spirit of God. Perhaps the way we understand God does not fit the experience of our spirit. This was the case for me. I used to see God in the old traditional way: as an old white-bearded man seated on the throne in heaven, looking down at me and judging my every move. He (and God most definitely was a "he") was authoritative and scary. He certainly was not a God of unconditional love nor was he personable. He was indifferent with me and was extremely disappointed if I had a single impure thought. I knew I was doomed to hell, and all I knew to do to win God's approval was prostrate myself on the floor begging for his forgiveness and hoping Jesus would advocate for me.

Many of you may have grown up seeing God in the same way. You may have lived in fear of God as I did. My friend, I want you to know that you do not need to debase yourself to be right with God. You are not required to approach God in fear (more on the difference between fear and faith in Chapter 7). Instead, all God requires is an open and receiving heart, and only then will God reveal Godself to you.

Words will always fall short of describing the indescribable God. God is indeed mysterious. Viewing God as a mystery rather than a fixed form sparks our innate human curiosity, motivating us to seek to know this mysterious God rather than hold back and dwell on our limited understanding. Viewing God as mystery opens our human vessel to receive from this mysterious God. Only through this receiving is God made manifest on this earthly plane. Let us not forget that we are vessels of God's continuous revelation.

If you ask the mystics to describe God, they would tell you as I have: it is an impossibility as God is indescribable. So how is one to explain God to another if God cannot be described? It is tough. Still, I want to attempt to describe to you the way I understand God after spending many years exploring God in various mystical traditions. Your understanding of God may be similar, or perhaps this will be a novel

> Inner silence is for our race a difficult achievement. There is a chattering part of the mind which continues, until it is corrected, to chatter on even in the holiest places.
>
> C.S. LEWIS

expression to you. There is value in seeing things in multiple perspectives, so take what you will out of the following description.

In the beginning was God and only God. Nothing else existed. No physical world. No mental world. No emotional world. No thoughts. No feelings. No sensations. No-*thing.*

Since no-*thing* existed but God, then God has to likewise be no-*thing.* God *is, was,* and *always will be* God apart from all things that can be thought, felt, or sensed. A Christian mystic living in the 14th century who penned *The Cloud of Unknowing* put it beautifully:

> *For He can well be loved, but he cannot be thought. By love He can be grasped and held, but by thought, neither grasped nor held. And therefore, though it may be good at times to think specifically of the kindness and excellence of God, and though this may be a light and a part of contemplation, all the same, in the work of contemplation itself, it must be cast down and covered with a cloud of forgetting. And you must step above it stoutly but deftly, with a devout and delightful stirring of love, and struggle to pierce that darkness above you; and beat on that thick cloud of unknowing with a sharp dart of longing love, and do not give up, whatever happens.*

God in God's eternal essence cannot be conceptualized. God in God's eternal essence cannot be felt. God in God's eternal essence cannot be heard, seen, tasted, smelled or touched. These expressions of our vessel are but secondary accounts of the true essence of God, which is indescribable. As soon as we attempt to conceptualize God, to feel God, or to sense God we automatically reduce God to the level of this human vessel. People have tried to conceptualize God through words, symbols, and religions but no word, symbol, or religion

Silence is God's first language.

ST. JOHN OF THE CROSS

can radiate the true wholeness of God's essence. This is why religion will always fall short of Divine access. God cannot be put in a doctrinal box or confined to a single location or religion. God cannot be personified or objectified, for personification and ob-

You are encircled by the arms of the mystery of God.

HILDEGARD OF BINGEN

jectification are idolizing concepts about God and neglecting the direct connection to the God of those concepts.

So how does one come to know God if God cannot be summed up in a thought, an emotion, or a sensation? How does one encounter God beyond the limitations of our human vessel? The Sons of Korah beautifully expressed what has proven to be an effective meditation of letting God reveal Godself to you without interference of our human vessel. They penned:

Be still and know I Am God. (Psalm 46:10)

This verse calls for an immediate presence with God. To know God in God's very essence, you must surrender yourself to the presence of God right here and right now. You must surrender all your thoughts about God, your feelings in response to God, and your sensations that may or may not be detecting God. You must let go of all formations and surrender to the God of the very beginning: the God of no-*thing*. You must find God in the stillness, between the thoughts and images; in this stillness between all things created, God can be found. Once you discover God in the stillness, you will discover God everywhere and in all things. You will discover God in organic and inorganic forms. You will discover God in the deserts, mountains, rivers, and seas. You will discover God in the prey, and you'll also discover God in the predator. You will discover God in the saint and in the sinner. You will discover

God in chaos and also in order. You will discover God in both the joys and in the sufferings of this life. As 14th century Christian mystic Julian of Norwich beautifully wrote:

> *The fullness of joy is to behold God in everything.*

Once you can see God in all things, you will find it unnecessary to put your confidence in any single conceptual understanding. When you shift in this perspective, you will begin to rely less on your own concepts and open yourself to the God that will lead you to more.

You are not your thoughts; you are a child of the mysterious God who desires to use you as a vessel of Godself. Remember the meditation:

> *Be still and know I am God.*

Reflection Questions

1. What are my concepts about God? Where did I get these concepts?

   _____

   _____

   _____

   _____

2. What concepts of God do I find most difficult to release?

   _____

   _____

   _____

   _____

3. What would it be like to see God as a mystery?

   _____

   _____

   _____

   _____

Prayer Practice

Close your eyes and focus on your breath. As thoughts enter your mind, notice them and then allow yourself to release them. If you experience an emotion or sensation, likewise notice it and release it. Do this until your vessel is at a state of internal peace. Then repeat the following words: *Be still and know that I am God.*

Sit in the silence, focused on these words. Sit in this silence for at least ten seconds. Then repeat the following: *Be still and know that I am.*

Like before, pause and sit in the silence. Then repeat: *Be still and know.*

Sit in the silence of the prayer. Then repeat: *Be still.*

Do as before. Then finally say: *Be.*

Sit in the silence of presence for as long as you are able. Then enter your prayer practice.

4

From Belief to Liberation:

How We View Salvation

CAM IVERSON was the town drunkard. Living at the time of prohibition, Cam led a life of crime. Not only was he a drunk, but his addiction steered him to join a town gang that frequently robbed houses and picked fights with random strangers on the streets. He was known as "Half-Pint Cam" because he could consume substantial amounts of alcohol. Town residents feared Cam, and avoided encountering him at all cost. He brought his troubling behavior into his childhood home and wreaked havoc on the lives of his parents and siblings. Eventually, he encountered the justice system and was sentenced to 1-3 years at Monroe Correctional Facility. Deeper and deeper into transgressions Cam fell. He was aware of his wrongdoing and deeply wanted to change his behavior, but nothing he did freed him of his addiction.

Then one Sunday morning Cam attended a church service. He took a seat in the back of the church so he would be the first one out the door when the service was over. But that Sunday morning there was a guest preacher, and towards the end of the service he pointed at Cam and said, "Son, you are under conviction!" Cam could not believe the audacity of the preacher to call him out! Cam's first response was, "No I'm not!" The preacher then went to Cam and pulled him towards the altar. He was furious and wanted to punch the preacher in the mouth.

Suddenly, hands were laid upon Cam and prayers were made to God. Cam's mom was in attendance, who wept as she witnessed the hand of God move Cam's heart. For years she had prayed that God would save her boy.

In the days that followed, Cam gave up drinking. He did not have a single craving for a drink. At that point he made the decision to stop his criminal undertakings, leaving the gang he had been affiliated with for many years. He stopped stealing from houses. He stopped fighting strangers on the street. He stopped smoking and cursing. He was a new man. He was saved from his wretched addiction, and he committed himself fully to serving the God that saved him. As he later recounted, Cam remembered the liberation created by his salvation experience.

I grew up taking my religion very seriously. I stood by what I believed and called out those who did not stand with me. I believed that in order to be saved one first had to believe Jesus died for their sins and utter a simple prayer:

Jesus, I ask you to be my Lord and Savior. Please forgive me for my sins.

That was it. By believing that Jesus died for your sins and asking Jesus for forgiveness, God welcomed you into his kingdom. You could remain a disturbed and vile person. You could still be living in constant fear and manifest little spiritual fruit. But as long as you had the correct beliefs and asked Jesus to forgive you for your sins, you were saved. Salvation was less a transformation in this life and more of a golden ticket to heaven when you died.

> **As we are liberated from our own fear, our presence automatically liberates others.**
>
> **NELSON MANDELA**

What is interesting is even though I was a religious Christian in those earlier years, I was in spiritual bondage. I believed I had the golden ticket to heaven, yet that golden ticket did little to comfort me or transform me in my present life. I lived in constant fear and anxiety, endlessly bombarded by the stresses of everyday life. It was not until years later that I experienced what I consider my real salvation experience, a deliverance from the prison of fear and anxiety.

What is Salvation?

The Hebrew word for salvation is *yesha* (this is the same base word for the Biblical names *Joshua* and *Jesus*). *Yesha* means freedom from what restricts, or what simply means deliverance. The Greek equivalent *soteria* means the same: deliverance or salvation. The word I think best describes both words is liberation.

To many religious Christians, salvation means liberation from sin, death, and eternal torment. To many practicing Jews, salvation means deliverance from suppression. Exodus gives us a clear example of this perspective, as the Hebrews were *delivered* from bondage in Egypt. During the Roman Empire, Jews were waiting for the coming Messiah to deliver them from the hands of political opponents. Salvation, deliverance, and liberation can all be used simultaneously. Healing also indicates a salvation experience, as was the case with my grandpa Cam.

For me, my salvation experience (my transition from religion to relationship) gave me a liberation like I had never experienced before. I was liberated from the fear and anxiety that kept me restricted for years. I

> The true value of a human being can be found in the degree to which he has attained liberation from the self.
>
> **ALBERT EINSTEIN**

gained the freedom to explore God in a variety of ways without fear. I experienced the love of God, and my fear vanished (1 John 4:18). I felt delivered from the slaveries of the mind and emotions. Then, the fruits of the spirit exploded in my life. Though trials continued to come, joy, peace, and patience were normalized in my life where before they were a rarity. I had been liberated from all that oppressed my spirit, and for the first time in my life I felt I had come to know God as my grandpa had.

Years ago I came across a word that built on my experience of salvation. The word is *metanoia*. In the original Koine Greek, *meta* means "after" or "beyond" and *nous* means "mind". Translated, *metanoia* means "beyond the mind" or a transformation of the mind. *Metanoia* is commonly used throughout the New Testament (Matthew 3:11, 9:13; Mark 1:4, 2:17; Luke 3:3, 3:8, 5:32, 15:7, 24:47; Acts 5:31, 11:18, 13:24, 19:4, 20:21, 26:20; Romans 2:4; 2 Timothy 2:25; Hebrews 6:6, 12:17).

There is also the word *metamelomai* which means "to repent" or "to regret". Some translate *metamelomai* to mean remorse or painful sorrow. *Metamelomai* is used in the Bible when describing Judas' repentance after betraying Jesus (Matthew 27:3). As the story goes, Judas had *metamelomai* and eventually committed suicide. *Metanoia* is written ten times more often in the Bible than *metamelomai*.

In the English translations of the Bible, *metanoia* and *metamelomai* were combined with the common translation of "repent". This merging was a grave mistranslation. Let us take a look at a mistranslated verse in Matthew's gospel that has often been quoted at the pulpit to justify the negative emotions of guilt, shame, and regret as prerequisites for salvation.

> Salvation lies not in the faithfulness to forms, but in the liberation from them.
>
> **BORIS PASTERNAK**

Repent, for the kingdom of God (or heaven) is at hand. (Matthew 4:17)

If you grew up in the church like me, you probably heard this verse many times. You likely believed that repentance was the first act you had to do to be saved. Some of you may have experienced crying out to God for forgiveness, in which you were immediately hit with a feeling of shame and painful regret. You believed this dark feeling to be a good thing, as a way to get God to accept you so you may have eternal life. In all likelihood, you battled with these feelings of guilt, shame, and regret for most of your Christian life, confused as to whether these feelings were good or bad. The religious understanding of salvation may have convinced you that you were saved (in the afterlife), but it likely did not deliver you from your present inequities.

Any psychologist can tell you the dangers of guilt, shame, and regret on a person's psyche. I remember when I meditated on the verse above in my early years I had constant anxiety and an extremely low sense of self-worth. It was normal to feel ashamed of myself. I was constantly failing to obey God's commandments, and though I considered myself "saved" I surely did not feel saved. Every hour that went by without me asking God for forgiveness would intensify my shame and lead me to once again repent. It was a continuous cycle with no end. I felt constantly on edge, walking on eggshells around God. Love, joy, and peace were words I frequently used but they were far from ripe in my life.

It may be surprising to learn that the word "repent" in Matthew 4:17 was mistranslated. When reading the English translation one could quickly assume that the Greek word *metamelomai* was used

> You're transforming old patterns of your mind and letting go of thoughts you don't need to have around any longer.
>
> ANONYMOUS

in this verse, but it was not. *Metanoia* was. So let us do something radical: let us change the translation to its original Greek meaning, shall we?

Transform your mind, for the kingdom of God is at hand.

Notice the difference. There is no hint of guilt, shame, and regret in this passage. There is no requirement to repent. Rather, John the Baptist called his followers to *transform their minds* because the kingdom of God was at hand. A modern translation may suffice:

Transform your mind and *you will see God.*

John's message was not a call for repentance but a call for transformation. Salvation requires absolutely no repentance. It requires an openness to be transformed and thus liberated by God.

The Process of *Metanoia*

In order to experience *metanoia*, an individual must first experience an awakening of the spirit. This is most often brought on by what Christians call "grace". It is not an awakening that can be initiated through our thoughts, feelings, or actions. Rather, it is by God's grace that an individual experiences it. The spiritual awakening brought on by the grace of God can be seen as an individual's first God-experience. It is like a seed planted by God directly into the heart, which then must be cultivated in order to awaken the entire individual. Once the initial awakening occurs,

> **Nothing happens until the pain of remaining the same outweighs the pain of change.**
>
> **ARTHUR BURT**

your conscious mind will begin the process of transformation, followed by your subconscious mind, and finally your behavior. This is the transformational process of *metanoia*.

Transformation literally means going beyond your form.

WAYNE DYER

When a person attempts to change their behavior first, they are working opposite to the process of *metanoia*. Because the person is working to correct their behavior before undergoing deeper levels of spiritual and mental transformation, that behavior will likely remain unchanged. This is why it is so difficult to correct bad habits. For years Cam tried to change his addictive behavior but with no success. Why? Because beneath the layers of destructive behavior were deeper levels of affliction that he had to address first. As I have come to witness in my own classroom, you cannot expect students to change their behavior unless their mental and emotional selves are worked with.

Deeper than the behavioral level is a person's subconscious or emotional level. Our emotions lie within the subconscious mind, and our behavior is often the manifestation of these emotions. As humans we experience both positive and negative emotions throughout the entirety of our lives. Emotions come and emotions go; emotions rise and emotions fall depending on any given situation. Therefore, a change of emotions does not necessarily mean an individual is transformed. This is why any emotional-based salvation experience fails to fully liberate an individual. If you base your salvation on an emotional experience, as many Christians do, you will eventually fall back to your former ways as soon as you experience emotional lows, which you certainly will. I have seen countless people fall on the altar crying out to God and *feeling* their way to salvation, to later regress back to their old, habitual ways. This is what irks me about mass conversions, as many churches and their leaders design their services to emotionally manipulate the congregation into thinking and feeling they are saved and to then use that experience as leverage for keeping those converts emotionally attached to their churches. That is not liberation. That is not salvation. It is manipulation. In contrast, Cam said he felt *nothing* during his salvation experience, yet he was wholly transformed. Emotions must be seen for what they are: not the doorway to salvation but as a window to the natural responses of our subconscious mind that indicate when there is something that needs to be resolved.

Beneath the behavioral and subconscious/emotional levels is a person's conscious level. It is here where *metanoia* is crucial. When one changes their conscious thoughts it has the potential to change one's emotions and subsequently their behavior. This is how people are able to successfully change their habits. Let me give you an example. I had a student several years back that had a very negative perception of herself. She consciously told herself she was a bad student, and as a result she had failing grades. Later that same school year, this student made a transformative change in her mind. She started to consciously think of herself as a strong academic student. This change did not occur quickly or naturally, and she had to intentionally work through several mental breakthroughs. Over time her self-talk changed. Instead of saying, "I suck at math" she started saying, "I may not understand this now, but I am growing." She not only said it to herself, but she started to *feel* the change. As a result, her grades went from F's to A's. At the end of the school year, she became one of my top ten students.

> I hate thinking about how many people have gone to church for decades and remain joyless or judgmental or bitter or superior.
>
> JOHN ORTBERG

Your mind is a powerful weapon that can either grow or deflate you. Even if your emotions and behavior are still troubled, by changing your conscious thoughts your emotions and behavior will soon follow, if the intention remains. The struggle for most of us is that we are still very much attached to certain patterns of thought that keep us bound. In order to change destructive thought patterns, we must become aware of how we think. This is what is called metacognition. By being cognizant of your thoughts and thinking patterns you create distance between those thoughts and patterns to be able to change them. This deeper level of awareness takes place "beyond the mind". This is *metanoia*. The Apostle Paul knew of the power behind our thoughts. As he said to the Philippians:

> Complacency is the deadly enemy of spiritual progress. The contented soul is the stagnant soul.
>
> AIDEN WILSON TOZER

> *Finally, brothers and sisters, whatever is true, whatever is noble, whatever is right, whatever is pure, whatever is lovely, whatever is admirable- if anything is excellent or praiseworthy- think about such things. (Philippians 4:8)*

A person may come to the altar physically, confess their sins emotionally, and believe Jesus died for their sins mentally. Yet, so often the individual remains unchanged. One can call themselves a Christian all they want and still remain stuck in their old destructive mental, emotional, and behavioral patterns. In other words, one can be a Christian and not be saved.

So how does one become saved? How does one become liberated in this life? I think it would be helpful for any Christ-follower to turn to the words of Jesus to find the answer. Let us look at three different passages from the Gospels: Luke 9:23-25, John 12:24-26, and Mark 2:21-22.

> *Then he said to them all: "Whoever wants to be my disciple must deny themselves and take up their cross daily and follow me. For whoever wants to save their life will lose it, but whoever loses their life for me will save it. What good is it for someone to gain the whole world, and yet lose or forfeit their very self?" (Luke 9:23-25)*
>
> *Very truly I tell you, unless a kernel of wheat falls to the ground and dies, it remains only a single seed. But if it dies, it produces many seeds. Anyone who loves their life will lose it, while anyone who hates their life in this world will keep it for eternal life. Whoever serves me must follow me; and where I am, my servant also will be. My Father will honor the one who serves me. (John 12:24-26)*
>
> *No one sews a patch of unshrunk cloth on an old garment. Otherwise, the new piece will pull away from the old, making the tear worse. And no one pours new wine into old wineskins. Otherwise, the wine will burst the skins, and both the wine and the wineskins will be ruined. No, they pour new wine into new wineskins. (Mark 2:21-22)*

Do you see a common message behind Jesus' three teachings here? Jesus said that whoever wants to save their life must first lose it. He said to be his follower of him we must "take up [our] cross." We must die to our old selves in order to live as a new self in Christ. This is not a physical death; it is an egoic one. To experience such a death, an individual must *let go* of their old identity and all the attachments to it. Jesus went even further to require some of his disciples to leave their families, as he knew this was where their attachments lay. He instructed the rich man to sell all his possessions and give the money to the poor and follow him, because he knew the rich man was attached to his possessions (Matthew 19:21). There are strong connections between Jesus' teachings here and the teachings of the Buddha, who also taught the importance of non-attachment in order to free yourself from the bondage of suffering. The message is the same: in order to experience salvation (aka enlightenment), you must die to your former self. When this happens, your consciousness shifts from your ego (that is, your thoughts) to your true center as a vessel of God. This is what is called being "born-again." This is salvation.

It is amazing watching how broken people gain a new freedom in Christ and are liberated from their struggles. Talk to any liberated person and they will tell you the freedom they have gained from their conscious shift. Yet for many of us, transformation stops here. Herein lies another problem.

The Parable of the Two Wanderers

The spiritual walk is like two wanderers in the desert, searching for a place to settle. Both wanderers know that in order to find such a place, they must locate a source of freshwater. The first wanderer comes across a small pond with a magnificent view. As the wanderer looks across the water he notices it is stationary and has an odd color. He is not sure how long the water has been sitting, but seeing several houses built around the pond, he reasons that the pond is an ideal location to live. Weak and weary of the long journey, the wanderer decides to settle in this place. For the rest of his life the wanderer lived on the pond with little movement. The pond provides food, but the stagnant waters provide little nutrition. The man struggles to survive and is often afflicted with sickness. Nevertheless, he remains at the pond. As other travelers pass by the pond, the wanderer tries to convince them to stay with him at the pond, promising life. Some were convinced to stay, weak and weary themselves. But most decide to travel on in order to find a better source of freshwater.

> When I let go of
> what I am, I become
> what I might be.
>
> LAOZI

The second wanderer traveled on for many days. He eventually comes across a spring.

He notices that the spring is flowing and very clear. He also notices a great deal of silt on the shores of the spring, left behind by the spring's seasonal floods. He imagines all the nutritious food he could grow on the silty ground, though it would be much work. The weak and weary wanderer decides this is the place to live. Over time the wanderer grows stronger and stronger. The spring provided constant freshwater and the grounds around the spring were used to grow food. Even though he had to frequently move his home when the seasonal floods came, the wanderer learned to utilize the floods to maximize his well-being. As other travelers passed by the spring, the second wanderer welcomed them in. Some decided to stay at the stream with him, setting up their own settlements and growing their own food. Most traveled on looking for greener pastures.

A Life of Continued Liberation

The parable of the two wanderers describes two very different Christian paths. I will call these two paths Stagnant Water Christianity and Living Water Christianity.

Stagnant Water Christianity is the Christian path dominated by religion. The Stagnant Water Christian may experience a form of liberation by becoming a Christian (resting their weary selves at the pond). After this initial liberation, the Stagnant Water Christian adopts, maintains, defends, and promotes their new pond of beliefs. These beliefs remain relatively the same for much of the Christian's life. To the Stagnant Water Christian, the pond is all there is. They fear to even glance at the greater environment around them, instead vowing to remain by their pond which they are familiar with and view anything outside the pond as dangerous. The Stagnant Water Christian understands the Great Commission to be a call to convince others to settle at their pond. Some decide to buy-in, but most decide to move on.

The Stagnant Water Christian is troubled by this, wondering why all spiritual seekers do not stay by the pond he or she has discovered.

You will never glory in God till first of all God has killed your glorying in yourself.

CHARLES SPURGEON

Living Water Christianity, on the other hand, is the Christian path of continued liberation. After salvation, the Living Water Christian may adopt a certain set of beliefs, but they remain open for new waters of revelation and the potential for old beliefs to change. Like a spring, the Living Water Christian's spiritual life is dynamic and flowing. They are in a continual process of evolution and replace old versions of themselves that no longer serve them. Like the silt next to the stream, on the former grounds of the old self is an opportunity for spiritual growth, enabling the Living Water Christian to cultivate abundant fruits such as love, joy, and peace within their lives and the lives of others. The more spiritual work done to the soil of the self, the greater the fruit production. When others approach the spring, the Living Water Christian encourages them to settle at the spring they have found. Some will take up the offer, opening themselves to a life of continuous liberation. Most, however, will choose to move on searching for what the stream has to offer.

When Jesus told his disciples to take up their crosses, he was not suggesting this was a one-time event. Instead, Jesus indicated it was a daily undertaking (Luke 9:23-25). Jesus further emphasized:

> *Salt is good, but if it loses its saltiness how can it be made salty again? It is fit neither for the soul, not the manure pile; it is thrown out. (Luke 14:34-35)*

The first ego death probably entailed some form of suffering as the old self fought to stay relevant. "Taking up your cross" is not a feel-good experience. Yet, it is through "the dark night of the soul" where one learns to let go of the old self and be reborn into a liberated creation. Nevertheless, that newly formed creation eventually becomes stale. As Jesus indicated, our salt loses its saltiness; our new wineskins become old. The only way to maintain the dynamic wine of Christ is to cast out the old wineskin and adopt a new wineskin once again. Transformation is not a one-time event but an ongoing process. We change as the world changes around us. When we fight that change we lose our effectiveness and inflate our ego, adding another unnecessary layer of bondage. To continue the journey of liberation, we must continuously and consciously let go of all attachments that no longer serve the dynamic wine of Christ. For those willing to undergo continuous wineskin replacements, you will start to develop a deeper sense of spiritual awareness beyond all forms of ego. The more wineskin replacements you undergo the better you learn to detach from these wineskins that often distract us from focusing on God. You begin to see that there is indeed a difference between the wineskins that you possess and the wine of Christ that's ever-flowing within you. Your concentration begins to center less on the wineskin that you are and more on the receiving of the wine itself. As you continue to open yourself, you will notice the emergence of spiritual fruits in your life, fruits such as love, joy, peace, patience, kindness, goodness, faithfulness, gentleness, and self-control (Galatians 5:22-23). There is no law, no rules and no religion that can manifest these fruits, only the open vessel. Jesus details this fruit even more:

> *I am the true vine, and my Father is the vinedresser. Every branch in me that does not bear fruit he takes away, and every branch that does bear fruit he prunes, that it may bear more fruit. Already you are clean because of the word that I have spoken to you. Abide in me, and I in you. As the branch cannot bear fruit by itself, unless it abides in*

the vine, neither can you, unless you abide in me. I am the vine; you are the branches. Whoever abides in me and I in him, he it is that bears much fruit, for apart from me you can do nothing. (John 15:1-17)

The old branches that do not bear good fruit are trimmed away by the internal Christ. The branches that do bear good fruit, on the other hand, are pruned and nurtured, further enabling the branch to grow and bear more fruit that can then be shared with others.

You can claim to be a Christian and not be saved. You can repent of your sins and remain the same miserable person as you always were. You can have all the knowledge of a theologian and refuse to "take up your cross daily". You can be ordained into the priesthood or pastor a church and bear little spiritual fruit. You can read your Bible, attend weekly church services, raise your hands in worship, fall on bended knee, pray, and believe all the church's doctrines and be enslaved to yourself. Yet, liberation is right around the corner. All you need to do is surrender yourself to God.

Reflection | *Questions*

1. How does seeing salvation as *liberation* change the way I see salvation?

_____

_____

_____

_____

_____

_____

2. How does replacing the word "repent" with the words "transform your mind" change the way I understand salvation?

_____

_____

_____

_____

_____

_____

3. Do I feel like I have had a salvation experience? If so, how did this experience liberate me?

_____

_____

_____

_____

_____

4. Which beliefs do I have difficulty *letting go* of? How does attachment to these beliefs restrict me from full liberation?

_____

_____

_____

_____

_____

5. What fruits are evident in my life today?

_____

_____

_____

_____

_____

Prayer Practice

During your prayer practice, choose one word to meditate on: the Hebrew word *yesha*, the Greek equivalent *soteria*, or the English equivalent *liberation*. As you are in prayer, when any thought enters your mind, allow the thought to express itself, repeat your chosen word and then let the thought go. When an emotion is triggered, do the same: allow the emotion to express itself, repeat your chosen word, and then release it to God. Do this until you are in a state of internal peace.

Then shift your focus to your various beliefs. Do the same as you did above: observe your thoughts and emotions in response to these beliefs. Allow them to be, repeat your chosen word, and then release them to God. Go through each of the beliefs you reflected on in the Reflection Questions. Finally, after you have gone through all your beliefs, shift your focus to God's presence. Surrender any thought or emotion to this Presence, and open yourself up to be spoken to.

5

From Disobedience to Opportunity:

How We View Sin

EVERY YEAR I do an activity with my students called "Famous Failures." The activity goes with my annual class theme of developing a growth mindset. I learned this activity from a fellow teacher. Let us see how you do!

The following is a list of famous celebrities. See if you can match their names to their life descriptions.

Michael Jordan	Walt Disney	J.K. Rowling
Abraham Lincoln	Albert Einstein	Elvis Presley

1. When she was in her 20s she was a divorced, poor, and unemployed single parent. She wrote a book in hopes of supplying for her family, but her book was rejected by all major publishers. _____

2. He failed to reach the required standard in the general education entrance exam. His teachers did not find him especially talented. He flunked math and was said to have had a learning disability. _____

3. After having his first on-stage performance his manager told him, "You ain't goin' nowhere, son. You ought to go back to drivin' a truck." _____

4. He was fired from a Missouri newspaper for lacking imagination and not being creative enough.

   _____

5. His mother died when he was nine, and his first love died when she was 26. He suffered a deep depression. His friends believed he was suicidal. _____

6. After failing to make his high school's varsity basketball team, he went home, locked himself in his room and cried.

   _____

How did you do? Let's see the results!

1. J.K. Rowling

2. Albert Einstein

3. Elvis Presley

4. Walt Disney

5. Abraham Lincoln

6. Michael Jordan

Students absolutely love this activity. In my classroom I have an entire wall display of twenty of these famous failures with a picture and a description of their failures. Every famous failure on the display went through some kind of difficult circumstance but used that circumstance as motivation for growth. They became the best at what they were criticized for, masters of what they previously failed at. It is encouraging watching these students scan the "Famous Failure" wall after having a rough day. I have witnessed countless students transition from a negative mindset of victimization to a growth mindset of intention.

What is Sin?

When you hear the word "sin", what is the first thing that comes to mind? To many of us, "sin" means a deliberate act of disobedience that angers God. Unless we confess our sin and ask God for forgiveness through the blood of Jesus Christ, God will judge us and send us to hell for eternity. Many others associate sin with evil. If you sin you are somehow working for the devil. However, this is far from the original meaning of sin. I believe as Christians it is paramount that we be reminded of what sin actually means, especially if we choose to use the word so freely.

The Greek translation of sin is *hamartia*, which means to "miss the mark." The same word is also used in archery. When the archer aims at the bullseye and misses, they *hamartia* or sin. Sin can therefore be understood as missing the mark of a particular target.

So the next question is, what is the target we are aiming at? In the Abrahamic traditions, that target is adhering to the religious law. Religious laws were not originally designed to test an individual's obedience to the laws. Rather, religious laws were created with the intent to bring about the highest state of consciousness (righteousness) of both the individual and society as a whole. In this highest state of consciousness, an individual and society could become the ultimate expression of God on earth.

> To sin is to be off the mark, that is, to inhibit development, contracting backward into regression rather than expanding forward into growth.
>
> CONNIE ZWEIG

Sin is the failure to do this. By sinning, an individual fails to make the invisible God visible. By sinning, an individual mishandles an opportunity to express God and ultimately give God the glory. Since God is love, we can think of sin as the failure to love. This includes both the failure to love God and/or the failure to love others. And you know something? We all sin! As Paul states in his letter to the Romans:

> *For all have sinned and fall short of the glory of God. (Romans 3:23)*

It does not matter if you are a serial killer or the Pope; all people sin because all people fail to be a perfect expression of love. As John the Evangelist says:

> *If we claim to be without sin, we deceive ourselves and the truth is not in us. If we confess our sins, he is faithful and just and will forgive us our sins and purify us from all unrighteousness. If we claim we have not sinned, we make him out to be a liar and his Word is not in us. (1 John 1:8-10)*

Jesus further emphasized that no one person is sinless in the story of the adulterous woman:

> *At dawn he appeared again in the temple courts, where all the people gathered around him, and he sat down to teach them. The teachers of the law and the Pharisees brought in a woman caught in adultery. They made her stand before the group and said to Jesus, "Teacher, this woman was caught in the act of adultery. In the Law, Moses commanded us to stone such women. Now what do you say?" They*

were using this question as a trap, in order to have a basis for accusing him.

> He that is without sin among you, let him first cast a stone at her.
>
> JOHN 8:7

But Jesus bent down and started to write on the ground with his finger. When they kept on questioning him, he straightened up and said to them, "Let any one of you who is without sin be the first to throw a stone at her." Again he stooped down and wrote on the ground.

At this, those who heard began to go away one at a time, the older ones first, until only Jesus was left, with the woman still standing there. Jesus straightened up and asked her, "Woman, where are they? Has no one condemned you?"

"No one, sir," she said.

"Then neither do I condemn you," Jesus declared. "Go now and leave your life of sin." (John 8:2-11)

I have heard people refer to this passage and focus solely on Jesus' last sentence: "Go now and leave your life of sin" as if the primary lesson in this story is a command to refrain from sin. This completely bypasses the central lesson in this story. Jesus was not teaching that we should refrain from sin. Jesus was teaching that no one was without sin, and therefore nobody has the right to judge the sin of another. He did not call out the adulterous woman, but rather called out the arrogant religious leaders who were accusing the adulterous woman. None of the leaders were able to step out and claim to be sinless, so they left baffled, pondering their own sin.

> Better a diamond with a flaw than a pebble without.
>
> CONFUCIUS

I feel it would be helpful to clarify Jesus' last words in this story. Jesus tells the woman, "Then neither do I condemn you." He subsequently tells her to "leave [her] life of sin." First of all, notice that Jesus did not condemn the woman as the religious leaders did. This differentiated him from those leaders, an obvious response of a man who valued relationship over religion. He was completely aware that the woman sinned against her husband, but he never condemned her for it. How fascinating is that? Instead, he instructed her to get rid of that (sin) which broke the bond of love between her and her husband. What a huge difference in the way we understand this story.

Let us dig into the concept of sin a little further. In the Gospel of Matthew, there is a passage Christians often use to justify judgment of a fellow Christian. Let's assess what Jesus said.

> *If your brother or sister sins against you, go and point out their fault, just between the two of you. If they listen to you, you have won them over. (Matthew 18:15)*

Once again, notice carefully what Jesus is saying here. Jesus did not say if your brother and sister sins, point out their fault. No, Jesus said if your brother and sister sins *against you* then go point out their fault. This is not a commandment to judge your brother or sister. This is a commandment to mend the love that was broken between two people. If you do something to offend another and that relationship is damaged, you are responsible for healing that bond. If you do something to a brother or sister and you are unaware of the damage you have caused, you would hope that a brother or sister would make you aware of this sin so that your relationship is not lost.

> I've failed over and over and over again in my life. And that is why I succeed.
>
> MICHAEL JORDAN

Sin is not a deliberate act of disobedience towards God. Sin is what stands in the way of perfect union with God, who is love. Perhaps we ought to start seeing sin in a more practical way: as an opportunity for spiritual growth.

Sin as an Opportunity for Spiritual Growth

American psychologist Carol Dweck coined the terms *fixed mindset* and *growth mindset* to compare two differing belief systems students have about their learning. Check out the chart below for a quick comparison of Dweck's two concepts.

Fixed Mindset	Growth Mindset
Avoid making mistakes	Learn from mistakes
Failure is seen as wrong	Failure is seen as an opportunity
Failure is feared	Failure is viewed as a challenge
Stuck in old habitual patterns	Modifies habits effectively
Looks for a scapegoat	Takes personal responsibility

A student with a fixed mindset is limited in their potential academic growth. A student who sees himself or herself as fixed in their ways remains stuck in the same old habitual patterns, never giving themselves the opportunity to make the necessary corrections. As a result, they experience the same failures over and over again. A student with a fixed mindset becomes a master of excuses. Instead of changing, they look for a scapegoat on which to place the blame of their failure. Until the student changes their mindset they remain stuck in these same patterns year after year.

A student with a growth mindset, on the other hand, experiences profound academic growth. They may experience the same failures as

> Success is not final,
> failure is not fatal:
> it is the courage to
> continue that counts.
>
> WINSTON CHURCHILL

the student with the fixed mindset, however, a student with a growth mindset will use those failures as growth opportunities. They may bomb a test in class but they keep their head held high, learning from their mistakes and progressing forward. When the next test comes, the student has grown, giving themselves a greater chance of improvement.

The major difference between a student with a fixed mindset and a student with a growth mindset is a student's *perception* of failure. The student who views failure as a bad thing or sees failure as inherent, will repeat that failure over and over again. The student who views failure as an opportunity for growth, on the other hand, learns from their failure, makes the necessary changes so they do not make the same mistakes, and grows to new levels of awareness.

One of the challenges I have noticed in middle school students is the fear of failure. Oftentimes this fear prevents them from even attempting their schoolwork. My students who have failing grades are not students who perform poorly on exams but rather ones who give up trying. The fear of failure is crippling. As author and spiritual teacher Paulo Coelho said:

> *The one who falls and gets up is stronger than the one who never tried. Do not fear failure but rather fear not trying.*

A teacher who encourages their students to avoid failure is ineffective. By teaching others to avoid failure, the teacher is setting their students up for a lifetime of anxiety, neglect, self-pity, and paranoia. No student is going to perform perfectly. Every student will struggle from time to time, even the most academically strong. In order to make the most out of failures, students must begin to see failure as a learning opportunity.

Let us translate the paragraph above to a Christian perspective. Instead of using the word "teacher" we will use the word "Christian" and instead of using the word "failure" we will use the word "sin".

> The one who falls and gets up is stronger than the one who never tried. Do not fear failure but rather fear not trying.
>
> PAULO COELHO

A Christian who encourages other Christians to avoid sin is ineffective. By telling others to avoid sin, the Christian is setting their peers up for a lifetime of anxiety, neglect, self-pity, and paranoia. No Christian is going to be sinless. Every Christian will sin from time to time, even the most righteous. In order to make the most out of sin, Christians must begin to see sin as a learning opportunity, as an opportunity to grow to their full potential as God expressions.

Trying to avoid sin makes you fearful. Conversely, striving for God builds your faith. The aim of the Christian life is to try to hit the bullseye as often as you can, but of course, you will miss from time to time. That's okay! As NBA legend Michael Jordan once said:

> *I've missed more than 9000 shots in my career. I've lost almost 300 games. Twenty-six times I've been trusted to take the game winning shot and missed. I've failed over and over and over again in my life. And that is why I succeed.*

Even the greatest of Bible characters, those who God spoke to, had their flaws.

Elijah was suicidal.

Gideon lived in fear.

Samson was a womanizer.

Rahab was a prostitute.

Noah was a drunkard.

Jacob was a cheater and a liar.

David was a murderer and adulterer.

Jonah ran from God.

Solomon was a sex addict.

Paul persecuted Christians.

Zacchaeus was money hungry.

Peter struggled with faith and denied Jesus three times.

Adam blamed others for his own fall.

Eve fell to temptation.

Sarah let her husband sleep with another woman and later resented her for it.

Moses was a murderer and had a bad temper.

Aaron created an idol.

Miriam was jealous and had greed for power.

Jesus was a heretic of his own religion.

> A person who never made a mistake never tried anything new.
>
> **ALBERT EINSTEIN**

Each of these Bible characters had obvious flaws (some may argue the case for a flawless Jesus). Yet, God used each character to bring about God's expression on earth. If God can use these characters to carry out God's plan, don't you think God can use you in all your flaws and weaknesses?

Sin is inevitable, even for the most righteous among us. Sin is a normal part of the human experience. Don not fret when you "miss the mark". Pick yourself up, take aim again, make the necessary corrections, and fire.

> Failure is only the opportunity to begin again more intelligently.
>
> HENRY FORD

When you do hit the mark, the reward will reveal itself.

Many Christians use Jesus as a scapegoat for redemption of their sin yet remain stuck in that sin. Many of us pray, "Jesus, please forgive me for my sins" and believe our sins are vanquished and think nothing more of it. As we go about our day we fall victim to the same sin over and over again. Many Christians use Jesus' death and sacrifice as a way to bypass transformation altogether. Christians need to approach sin differently. Instead of asking Jesus to merely forgive us of our sins (which has already been done), perhaps we ought to start asking Jesus to help us learn from our sins so that we may grow spiritually. Perhaps our prayers ought to be something like this: "Jesus, I acknowledge *this* sin in my life. Help me to grow from this sin and transform me into a better vessel of love." Trust that God is big enough to use your sin to mold you into a greater vessel of God's expression.

It is time for Christians to shift their mindset from seeing sin as an act of disobedience and start seeing sin as an opportunity to grow into spiritual maturity.

May your flaws project you forward.

> Failing forward is the ability to get back up after you've been knocked down, learn from your mistake, and move forward in a better direction.
>
> JOHN C. MAXWELL

Reflection Questions

1. How has my perspective of sin influenced the way I view myself? God? Others? The world?

_____

_____

_____

_____

_____

_____

2. How would viewing sin as "missing the mark" change how I respond to sin?

_____

_____

_____

_____

_____

_____

3. In what ways am I "missing the mark" in my relationship with God?

_____

_____

_____

_____

_____

_____

4. In what ways am I "missing the mark" in my relationships with others?

_____

_____

_____

_____

_____

_____

Prayer   Practice

Before your prayer practice, create a list of sins that you struggle with. Write these sins down in your prayer notebook and have them available during your prayer.

During your prayer practice, focus on each of the sins you wrote down and ask yourself this question: how has this sin prevented me from being or expressing love? Allow your heart and your mind to express themselves. Write these down if you find it necessary. Observe and acknowledge each of these expressions. Then surrender the sin to God. Release it, and allow God to overtake you. Finally, ask God to use this sin to grow you.

6

From Fear to Faith:

How We View the Unknown

THE FOLLOWING INFORMATION *was presented in Miceal Ledwith's documentary "How Jesus Became the Christ: The Hidden Years."*

In ancient Egypt there was a double temple called the Temple of Kom Ombo. The eastern half of the temple was dedicated to the crocodile god Sobek, who represented humanity's carnal nature. The western half of the temple was dedicated to the god Horus, who represented humanity's divine nature. Both halves were perfectly symmetrical, with identical entrances, halls, and sanctuaries. In the Ptolemaic period, initiates of the Egyptian mystery schools would enter the eastern half of the Temple of Kom Ombo. As they continued on into the inner chamber they came to a pool. In the pool was a float of crocodiles. They were told that at the bottom of the pool there was a hidden tunnel. The initiates were then asked to jump into the pool, find the tunnel, and swim through it. The initiates responded in two different ways. Some initiates who jumped into the pool were overcome with fear, and they frantically splashed around and were devoured by the crocodiles. Other initiates jumped into the pool, maintained their composure, swam to the bottom of the pool and found the tunnel, which they swam into. As they continued through the tunnel they noticed a light at the end (no pun intended!). When they reached the end of the tunnel they realized

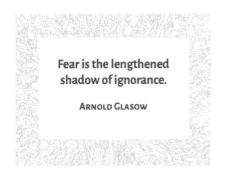

Fear is the lengthened
shadow of ignorance.

ARNOLD GLASOW

they had come out on the western half of the inner sanctuary of the temple of Horus. Here they were initiated into the Egyptian mystery school.

The initiates who responded in fear were eaten by the crocodiles, while the initiates who remained calm trusted there was hope at the other end of the tunnel. All initiates had one thing in common: they jumped into the unknown waters.

Reactionary Fear vs. Residential Fear

Throughout our lives we encounter unknown waters. For many of us, this gives us increased anxiety. We do not like to be in the unknown. It presents potential dangers that are outside our control, which is why many of us decide to keep within our comfort zones and avoid the unknown altogether. It seems reasonable to stay within one's comfort zone of experience, where things are familiar. Yet, there are times in our lives where we have no choice but to enter the unknown waters. Our first human response is oftentimes fear, which cripples us from action and prevents us from walking the path ahead. It is this fear I would like to assess.

There are two kinds of fears that we experience as humans: reactionary fear and residual fear. Reactionary fear is our oldest instinctual response. All animals are driven by reactionary fear. This keeps them safe when they sense danger. When a deer senses danger, reactionary fear tells it to run into the forest. When a skunk senses danger, reactionary fear tells it to spray. When an opossum senses danger, reactionary fear tells it to play dead (though I always wondered how this was an effective strategy!). Humans have inherited this same reactionary response. Reactionary fear, activated by the amygdala, enables a person to respond quickly to a potential threat. It tells a person to step out of the way of a speeding car. It advises a person to stop before they approach a cliff's edge. Reactionary fear is necessary for our survival. After the danger has withdrawn, adrenaline recedes and our body, mind, and emotions go back to a state of equilibrium called homeostasis.

Residual fear is similar to reactionary fear in that the amygdala is activated the same way, alerting the body of potential danger. Unlike reactionary fear, however, residual fear occurs whether or not there is a real threat present. Residual fear can be triggered by a single thought or memory. Because our thoughts dominate our lives, most fear that humans experience is residual fear. Unlike reactionary fear where the body, mind, and emotions go back to a state of homeostasis, residual fear often keeps the body-mind-emotions in a constant fear-response mode. This stresses the body-mind-emotions and creates imbalance. Without proper intervention, this imbalance will lead to the deterioration of a person's mental, physical, and emotional health and open them to the real possibility of sickness, disease, and even an early death.

Let me give you an example of residual fear. When I was in middle school I had a fear of talking to girls my age. I had gained a reputation as a shy boy, a reputation I did not like. During middle school dances, whenever a slow song came up I sprinted into the gym to play basketball because I did not want to dance with a girl. It was not until one of my girl friends literally grabbed my arm during a slow dance and made me dance with her that I was able to break past my fear of girls. This fear I had was silly and unnecessary. There was no real threat to my life. It was clearly residual fear.

> **Fear defeats more people than any other one thing in the world.**
>
> RALPH W. EMERSON

To further compare reactionary fear with residual fear, reflect on the chart below.

Reactionary Fear	*vs.*	**Residual Fear**
Natural		Unnatural
Rational		Irrational
Necessary		Unnecessary
Temporary		Long-Lasting
Real danger		Imagined danger

Within our Christian theology, we have incorporated elements of residual fear. In many Christian circles, fear is even seen as a holy virtue. Yet, one has to ask the question: is fear really required to know God? That question we will tackle next.

Must We Fear God?

If you are a Christian, you have likely pondered the concept of fearing God. Many of us who have grown up in the church have come to believe that it is a good thing to fear God. We classify this as "Godly fear". As a result, many of us are stuck in a constant state of residual fear.

> The cave you fear to enter holds the treasure you seek.
>
> JOSEPH CAMPBELL

I remember carrying this fear of God with me throughout my childhood. Eventually it turned into paranoia. Every ten minutes or so I would stop and ask God to forgive me of my sins in case Jesus were to return the next moment and God would punish me. I feared that if the rapture happened without asking for forgiveness of any sin I committed since my last confession, then my heart would not be right with God, and I would be left behind with all non-Christians. This fear gave me constant anxiety and guilt.

Scripturally, the fear of God is a contradiction. God's very nature is love, according to John the Evangelist, and perfect love casts out fear (1 John 4). If this is true, then fear is not only unnecessary to know God but it is against God's very nature. Yet, our conscience is split. There are numerous passages in the Bible (most notably in the Old Testament) where the authors encouraged the fear of God. Christians explain this to be a "Godly" fear. Fear and love are contradictory, and yet we are instructed to do both. It seems our only option is to pick and choose which verses we want to emphasize. Why somebody would choose fear over love is beyond me.

So, which are we supposed to do, fear God or love God? Where did this idea of fearing God even come from? I think it would help us to take a look at the history of this concept.

In the ancient world it was customary for people to fear their deities. Whether it was the ancient Mayans or Aztecs or the civilizations of ancient Egypt, Mesopotamia, and Greece, there is significant evidence to show that ancient cultures lived in perpetual fear of their gods and goddesses. This fear was lodged deep in the subconscious minds of the earliest civilizations.

Most ancient deities elicited a mixed bag of human emotions. Indeed, we made gods in our own image. One year these personified gods would be pleased with you and bless you and your family with a bountiful harvest. The following year the

> Everything you want is on the other side of fear.
>
> JACK CANFIELD

gods would be so angry with you that they would cause a great famine in the land as punishment. The ancients believed that calamity was the result of human wrongdoing that offended the gods in some way. In response, these cultures created specific sets of rules and guidelines aimed to stay on good terms with these teetering gods. This most often manifested as blood sacrifices. The gods clearly had issues with emotional regulation and needed humans to fear them to make them feel better about themselves!

This ancient mindset of fearing the gods also applied to the kingdoms of Israel and Judah. The writers of the Old Testament reveal that Yahweh is a God to be feared and sacrificed to. Yahweh was frequently angered by the actions of his people, especially those who worshiped other gods. After all, Yahweh was a jealous God, and as punishment for their adultery, he allowed famines in the land and outsiders to invade. To stop the wrath of Yahweh and amend for possible wrongs, Yahweh required blood sacrifices to be made to him (usually animal sacrifices but sometimes human sacrifices). For hundreds if not thousands of years this was common religious practice. Eventually this mentality found its way into Christianity and the development of atonement theology, where Jesus was seen as the final blood sacrifice to this angry Yahweh.

In the modern era, the concept of fearing the deities has mostly gone away. Still, this residual fear still permeates many religious traditions today, most notably the Abrahamic religions. In Christianity in particular, this fear still haunts its adherents. Even after Jesus presented us with an alternative understanding of God as love and forgiveness, many Christians still have a subconscious fear that God's judgment is somehow greater than God's love and thus fear is held to some higher spiritual value. The ancient concept of fearing God needs a radical exorcism. In an attempt to modernize the concept of fearing God, Pope Francis gave a description of what *fearing God* may actually mean:

The fear of the Lord, the gift of the Holy Spirit, doesn't mean being afraid of God, since we know God is our Father that always loves and forgives us. It is no servile fear, but rather a joyful awareness of God's grandeur and a grateful realization that only in Him do our hearts find true peace.

> There is no fear in love. But perfect love drives out fear, because fear has to do with punishment. The one who fears is not made perfect in love.
>
> 1 JOHN 4:18

Maybe instead of teaching our little ones to fear God, we ought to start teaching our little ones how to have *faith*.

Faith: Trusting God

The image of faith has been restricted in many modern Christian circles to merely mean belief. For years I thought that if you mentally "believe" in Jesus as your Savior you will be saved from God's judgment. Faith was principally a head action, a "certainty" of belief. Belief falls exceptionally short when describing faith:

Whereas belief arises from the *head*, faith arises from the *heart*.

Whereas belief focuses on the *seen*, faith focuses on the *unseen*.

Whereas belief is what you *know*, faith is trusting God in the *unknown*.

Whereas belief needs *evidence*, faith simply *trusts*.

> Cast all your anxiety on Him because He cares for you.
>
> 1 PETER 5:7

Whereas belief shines in the *light*, faith grows in the *darkness*.

Belief does very little in eliminating fear and guiding your spirit in the unknown. It often ignores fear and buries it deep beneath the conscious mind. Faith, on the other hand, acknowledges that fear and gives it directly to God. As one acronym of faith describes:

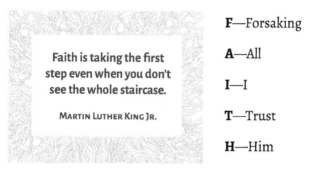

> Faith is taking the first step even when you don't see the whole staircase.
>
> MARTIN LUTHER KING JR.

F—Forsaking

A—All

I—I

T—Trust

H—Him

To transition from fear to faith when responding to the unknown, one must *let go* of fear and *let God* take the lead.

Moving from Fear to Faith

In Stephen Covey's book *The Seven Habits of Highly Effective People*, Covey introduced a concept called the *Circle of Concern*.

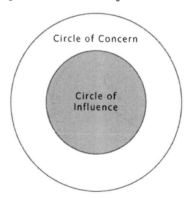

The *Circle of Concern* is a strategy used to help identify one's fears and whether or not they are necessary to focus on. Shown in the image above, the inner circle is the *Circle of Influence*. The *Circle of Influence* is the circle where one records fears that are within one's control. For example, if my child is walking in the middle of the parking lot with cars coming in and out, I hold the responsibility of taking that child out of that situation. The outer circle is the *Circle of Concern*, which contains both the fears of the Circle of Influence and the fears outside the Circle of Influence. The fears in the outer circle are fears that one cannot control. For example, many of us fear death. Though we can prolong our lives based on healthy choices, death is inevitable. Thus, worrying about death is unnecessary because it will come regardless.

All fears within the *Circle of Influence* are residual fears one can do something about. The fears outside the *Circle of Influence* are out of one's control and if one wants to address these fears they must surrender them to God in faith. As Jesus said:

> *Can any of you by worrying add a single hour to your life? (Matthew 6:27)*

Once you trust God with your fears, you will come to experience a profound peace that will only grow over time. As Paul encouraged the Philippians:

> *Do not be anxious about anything, but in every situation, by prayer and petition, with thanksgiving, present your requests to God. And the peace of God, which transcends all understanding, will guard your hearts and your minds in Christ Jesus. (Philippians 4:6-7)*
> Insert 6.8 Quote on side

Below is a practice that you may find helpful in your transition from a fear-based approach to a faith-based approach. I encourage you to try the practice and discover the benefits it has for your spirit. The first three steps are focused on becoming aware of your fears and the necessary actions to address the fears you can. The next two steps focus on letting go of the fears out of your control and letting God guide you through faith. The last step is an active remembrance of who you are in relation to God.

1. **Reflect.** In a journal, reflect and respond to the following five questions:

   What fears am I holding onto?

   Which fear has the most impact on my life?

   How does this fear limit me?

   What created this fear within me in the first place?

   When does this fear usually show itself?

2. **Recognize.** Awareness is key to moving beyond your fear. Acknowledge your fear when it comes up in your life. Call the fear out when it shows its face. By becoming consciously aware of your fear, you have done the biggest work of loosening fear's grip on your life.

> Faith is deliberate confidence in the character of God whose ways you may not understand at the time.
>
> OSWALD CHAMBERS

3. **Respond.** Act when necessary to those fears within your *Circle of Influence.* If you are afraid of being in large groups, take the first action step and join a small group. If you fear your spouse or loved one is upset with

you, initiate a conversation with them and discuss what is on your heart. Take action when necessary so the fear is addressed then and there and does not bury itself within you. Strive for homeostasis. When the fear you hold is outside your control, move to the fourth step.

4. **Release.** What seems like the easiest step is perhaps the most challenging. Release all control to God. Your ego will fight you! Recognize it, and release it. Remember: worry leaves little room for faith. "Cast all your anxiety on him because he cares for you (1 Peter 5:7). *Let go* of your fear and *let God* take the lead. The freedom gained with this step is beyond words. A huge weight will be lifted off your shoulders and your faith in God will deepen.

5. **Rely.** Repeat the FROG prayer:

   Fully

   Rely

   On

   God

> Fear is the glue that keeps you stuck. Faith is the solvent that sets you free.
>
> SHANNON L. ALDER

Display the FROG prayer in your home. Meditate on the words. Make it your mantra. This is the prayer that will grow your faith while in the unknown. It requires no action on your part but only patience. Wait for God's guidance to lead you.

6. **Remember.** Remember who you are. You are a vessel of God, and God has a purpose for you in your present struggles. As God told the prophet Jeremiah, "'For I know the plans I have for you,' declares the Lord. 'Plans to prosper you and not to harm you. Plans to give you hope and a future.'" Know that God is working something in and through you!

Pray, and let God worry.

MARTIN LUTHER

We cannot see God's master plan. We may not even sense God's presence. Nevertheless, when we enter the unknown waters there is a grand opportunity to grow our faith in God. As your faith continues to grow, you will find it easier to let go of the former fears that once possessed you and trust God completely in your own unfolding. When this happens, the unknown will no longer be a scary venture but an exciting journey.

Fear and faith are two different responses to entering the waters of the unknown. The real question is: what will your response be?

Reflection Questions

1. What fears am I holding onto?

_____

_____

_____

_____

2. How has fear limited my faith?

_____

_____

_____

_____

3. What would life look like if I started to truly live in faith?

_____

_____

_____

_____

Prayer Practice

Before your prayer practice do the following:

Draw a circle. Within that circle draw a smaller circle.
Label the large circle *The Circle of Concern* and label the
small circle *The Circle of Influence.* Outside of the circles
list all your fears. Think of as many as you can. Once
listed, start organizing your fears into two categories:
fears that you have control over and fears you have no
control over. Take the fears that you have control over
and place them inside the *The Circle of Influence.* Then
take the fears you have no control over and place them
inside *The Circle of Concern.* Cross out the title *The Circle
of Concern* and write *God's Territory* in its place. As you
are in your prayer practice, address each fear. Start with
the fears in *God's Territory.* As you contemplate each fear,
surrender it to God and ask God to fill you with faith
every time you experience this fear. Then contemplate
on the fears in *The Circle of Influence.* Ask God to reveal
solutions to these fears. Be open and ready to receive
guidance. Once you receive it, make a plan to address
these fears.

7

From Paradise to Presence:

How We View Heaven and Earth

GROWING UP, I viewed the world through the lens of the rapture. Questions drove my daily musings, questions such as, "When will Jesus return?", "Will I be raptured to heaven?" and "Will my loved ones make it?" My worldview was that our purpose on earth was to spread Christianity to the ends of the earth so that when Jesus does return they would be saved and go to heaven. If one did not accept Jesus as their personal savior, that person would be left behind to suffer through the seven year tribulation, which would eventually climax with the inevitable destruction of the world by fire. Those who still refused to accept Jesus during the tribulation would subsequently be destroyed with the world. The world was seen as going to hell, so the best thing one could do was put all attention on the afterlife. This worldview led me to fear for my own soul and fear for the souls of others.

As we transitioned into the new millennium, there was much talk in the media (and from my friends and family) that Jesus' return was near. My cousin and I found this very exciting. We anxiously awaited, spiritually preparing ourselves so we were stainless in the eyes of God in that very moment of rapture. I remember when the clock struck twelve and the new year hit, nothing happened. My cousin and I were greatly disappointed. We knew we were wrong about the timing, and now the thought haunted us that we now had to re-enter back into the world with the potential of our friends mocking us. But then a thought occurred to me, "I am only 12 years old; my life is just getting underway! I am glad Jesus did not return. I have so much to live for. Why would I want Jesus to return right now, anyway?"

These questions got me reflecting on how I was raised. My grandpa believed Jesus was going to return in his lifetime, that he was going to be raptured before he experienced death. Countless Christians before and after him have thought the same thing. People live and people die, yet the world remains as it has for 4.5 billion years.

The Carelessness of an Afterlife Focus

Why do some Christians focus so much on the afterlife? For older people like my grandpa it makes sense. He was nearing the end of his life. If he could escape death, awesome! As you near the end of your life you begin to reflect more on what comes after. For the first Christians it made sense as well. They witnessed Jesus' death and resurrection and seriously believed in his literal return to earth during their lifetimes when he would overthrow the Roman Empire and establish the authority of Israel once again. Of course, this never happened.

> Live in the present, launch yourself on every wave, find eternity in each moment.
>
> HENRY DAVID THOREAU

For me, my desire for Jesus' return disillusioned me. I loved my life. I loved creating new memories. I constantly daydreamed about my future and the future of the world. After experiencing the transition to the year 2000, I was glad to still be here. I then began to question why we as Christians focus so much on the afterlife and choose to ignore our life here and now.

The concept of an afterlife has been in the human consciousness since the development of the frontal lobe. As humans, we all desire to live a long life and most of us wonder

> If you are depressed, you are living in the past; if you are anxious, you are living in the future; if you are at peace, you are living in the present.
>
> LAO TZU

if that life will extend after we die. I personally believe there is life after death, although I cannot say what that life will look like. There are multiple views of the afterlife, ranging from culture to culture. Many of these perspectives are based on people's near-death experiences. Some near-death experiences radiate Christian imagery. A myriad of people have recorded their experience of seeing angels and heaven's pearly gates. Others have recorded their experiences of encountering hell and demons. In other religious traditions, people have recorded being in eternal bliss and experiencing unconditional love. Near-death experiences across religions and cultures describe how the experiencer saw deceased loved ones. Still others tell how they did not see anything. With so many differing near-death experiences it is difficult to claim only one to be right. I believe we gravitate towards the imagery that we are familiar with in our own religious tradition. We won't truly know what the afterlife will look like until we die and experience the transition to the spirit world for ourselves.

This for many Christians is not satisfactory. Many want a guarantee of the afterlife to ease their anxiety. Many Christians, in fact, arrogantly assume they already know what the afterlife will be like. To them, their perceived picture of the afterlife is the only true reality. Therefore, daydreaming about this afterlife is better than focusing on this broken world. To many of them, this world is dominated by Satan.

This is where a major problem lies. By focusing so much of our attention on the afterlife one begins to mentally and emotionally withdraw from stewardship of the earth. One can justly say that the afterlife focus is what is leading to the world's pending global downfall.

Reflect on this: if you are wrong about Jesus coming back within your lifetime, and you do not make any attempt to steward and better care for this earth now, your kids, grandkids, and descendants will inherit the same world you decided to neglect. Is that the legacy you wish to leave behind?

There are a minority of Christians, however, who see heaven and the earth in a totally different light.

Jesus Brought Heaven *to* Earth

Former pastor and author Brian McLaren once brilliantly said, "The gospel is not an evacuation plan for heaven. It's a transformation plan." If only we saw the gospel in this way! Jesus did not come into the world to condemn the world but to save it through himself (John 3:17). When his disciples asked him how to pray, Jesus told them:

Thy kingdom come, thy will be done, on earth as it is in heaven. (Matthew 6:10)

> Do not dwell on the past; do not dream of the future; concentrate the mind on the present moment.
>
> BUDDHA

Jesus not only brought the light of heaven to earth through his earthly ministry, but he guided his disciples to be fellow vessels in the continuation of this heavenly manifestation on earth. Jesus revealed to his followers a new divine level of consciousness that was to be generated on earth after his death. Through this new consciousness, the earth would be transformed in love, meaning God would reign on earth forever. Perhaps we ought to heed the advice of one of the most popular Bible characters, King David. As David said:

> The only thing that is ultimately real about your journey is the step you are taking at this moment. That's all there ever is.
>
> ECKHART TOLLE

The earth is the Lord's and all that is in it, the world, and those who live in it. (Psalm 24:1)

My friend, the earth does not belong to Satan, it belongs to God. When God created the world God declared it to be good six times (Genesis 1:4, 10, 12, 18, 21, 25, 31). In Genesis 1:31 God went even further to declare the earth as *very good*. When humans were created, God instructed us to appreciate and steward all of creation. This was God's first commandment to mankind (Genesis 2:15).

There is little support in Genesis that the earth is bad. Yes, there is sin. Yes, there is pain. Yes, there is suffering. Yes, there is death. None of these realities change the fact that the earth is God's. God never declared the earth to be bad. The problem is not the earth; the problem is mankind's destructive mindset.

All this leads to a suggestion: instead of putting all attention on the afterlife, which will come regardless if it is dwelled upon or not, perhaps we ought to put our focus on bettering the earth here and now. Perhaps instead of thinking about paradise, we ought to think about presence. As the author of Psalm 118 encouraged:

> *This is the day that the Lord has made; let us rejoice and be glad in it. (Psalm 118:24)*

By shifting our focus to our present life here,
several benefits will emerge:

1. You will value the earth and all its inhabitants.

We are extremely blessed to live here. So far, earth is the
only verified planet that can sustain life. All life is here for
but a brief segment of time, to live, to breathe, to express,
to create. There is so much diversity on this planet, and we
are all interconnected. By being present, we return to this
connection. By being present, we return to God's original
intention of the Sabbath: appreciating the Earth God created.

2. You will create deeper and more meaningful relationships.

I absolutely love to spend time with my two daughters,
Eily and Emmy. Even so, I often find my mind wandering
elsewhere when I am with them. When the time has
passed, I realize I wasted an opportunity to be fully present
with my girls. It kills me every time.

What a difference presence makes. When you are present,
you begin to find value in every moment you are blessed to have with your loved ones. By being present, you are free to love them and accept them for exactly who they are in that moment, without judgment. By being present, loving others is possible.

> That is why those who
> are not capable of being
> there in the present
> moment, they don't
> really live their life- they
> live like dead people.
>
> THICH NHAT HANH

3. Past depression and future anxiety disappear.

This one was a relief for me after four long months of depression. I tried everything to alleviate my suffering, but nothing worked. Then one day I decided to focus consciously on a single step. As I took that step I focused only on that step and nothing else. What I experienced was the most profound relief I had in months. This encouraged me to continue to grow my presence in all actions, and in every instance my depression was lifted. Eventually I was near-present in everything I did, and my depression eventually vanished.

> If you think your afterlife will be better than your current life, you're not really living. You're just waiting to die.
>
> UNKNOWN

4. You will manifest the fruits of the Spirit.

You do not have to wait for the afterlife to experience the fruits of the Spirit. Love, joy, peace, patience, kindness, goodness, faith, gentleness, and self-control (Galatians 5:22-23) can all be experienced right here and right now. To experience them, you must be present. Test it out for yourself. See how presence can bring forth the spiritual fruits you have been longing for in your life.

5. You will experience healing.

There were many supernatural healings on the Iverson family farm due to the faith of my great-grandma, Anna. One morning the Iverson cows were eating potatoes. One jersey cow named Dixie began to eat the potatoes, and suddenly a potato got caught in her throat. She was unable to swallow it, choked and fell over. When Anna's husband, Carl, realized what had happened, he rushed to his car and drove one mile into town to get the vet. Anna understood that by the time Carl came back with the vet it would be too late. So she went out to the field where the cow laid and became present with her. She then placed her hand on the cow's throat and shouted, "In the name of Jesus, potato go down!" The potato immediately went down, and the cow got up and went off grazing.

How did this miracle happen? Anna declared healing in Jesus' name in that present moment. She did not say, "God, if you can heal my cow, I would really appreciate it" (future thought). She did not say, "Oh no, I didn't cut the potatoes up small enough!" (past thought) No. She declared in that moment that God was healing the cow. By being present, God was able to use Anna as a vessel of healing.

6. You receive clarity of your mission.
Ecclesiastes 9:10 says:
Whatever your hand finds to do, do it with all your might,
for in the realm of the dead, where you are going, there is neither
working nor planning nor knowledge nor wisdom.

You were not put here on this earth to waste your life away thinking about what comes after. You have a purpose for being here. You are a unique creation of God, full of strengths, passions, dreams, ideas, and insights that are directly tied to your life mission. Embrace this mission! Not only will you be aligned with your truest nature; others will reap the benefits as well.

7. **You will experience God.**

God is not just some ancient deity of the past or the victorious deity of the future. God is God of the *now* and always has been and always will be. God is not bound by space or time, nor does God need space or time to be experienced. The present moment transcends both space and time. The present moment *is*, just as God *Is*. When Moses asked God in the burning bush who was speaking, God replied, "*I Am Who I Am*" (Exodus 3:14). God did not say "I was *this*" or "I will be *that*." We use the word *presence* for a reason when describing the spirit of God. You do not have to wait for the afterlife to experience God. You can experience God's presence here and now.

All of us have lost loved ones that we want to see again. I believe we will. Perhaps they are even amongst us now in some mysterious way. Regardless, the hope to see them should not take away from our present life. You can believe in an afterlife and not be consumed by it. You can be prepared for Jesus' return and still live presently every day, every hour, every minute, and every second. We must be prepared for anything and ready to adjust in every given moment. You do not have to wait to go to heaven to experience God's love. You can experience heaven right here and right now on earth.

> Jesus's resurrection is the beginning of God's new project not to snatch people away from earth to heaven but to colonize earth with the life of heaven. That, after all, is what the Lord's Prayer is about.
>
> NT WRIGHT

Reflection Questions

1. What benefits am I gaining by focusing on the afterlife?
    How can I get these same benefits while living presently?

    _____

    _____

    _____

    _____

    _____

    _____

2. What benefits would I gain if I shifted my focus to the
    present moment?

    _____

    _____

    _____

    _____

    _____

    _____

3. Do I tend to regret the past or worry about the future? How can I be more present?

_____

_____

_____

_____

_____

4. What are some things I can do today to better steward the world?

_____

_____

_____

_____

_____

5. What would my relationships look like if I was more present?

_____

_____

_____

_____

_____

Prayer *Practice*

In Hebrew, the word "ruach" means *breath, wind* or *life force*. The Greek equivalent "pneuma" means *breath* or *spirit*. Essentially, spirit and breath are the same thing. When God breathes life into you, God gives you God's spirit. As you give your last breath, you give that spirit back to God.

Find someplace to sit down outside. Close your eyes and begin to focus on your breath. Do this for several minutes. When your mind starts to wander (and it will), bring your focus back to your breath. This is your spirit. This is your connection to the eternal God. When you are ready, open your eyes and begin to observe the world around you. Be present with everything you are experiencing. How diverse and fascinating the earth is! You may decide to get up and move around. If possible, walk around barefoot, connecting your feet to the earth. This is known as grounding. Be present in every footstep. Engage in every moment. Do this as often as you can. As your present awareness grows, the benefits of presence will reveal themselves in your life.

8

From Closed Book to Open Revelation:

How We View God's Word

THROUGHOUT HER CHILDHOOD in Norway and her adulthood in the United States, my great-grandmother, Anna Iverson, faithfully attended church services. She was passionate about growing her relationship with God, and she was continuously open for God's revelation and calling in her life. When tribulations unfolded in her household, her church failed to comfort and support her. Yet, Anna's faith in God grew to rare levels. Her son Hegge recorded the following story:

> Mother didn't turn into a spiritual giant overnight. When she found out that her husband was not only drinking heavily, but was also cheating on her, she was heartsick. Then she saw the children going the same way—cursing, drinking, staying out late—and she was shattered. I often heard her crying in hopeless frustration. Slowly, slowly, she had to let God teach her the reason for her afflictions.
>
> One day Mother cried out to the Lord, "Why am I in this terrible darkness?"
>
> "So you will learn to know Me and trust Me," came the answer. "I have wonderful things to teach you."
>
> As she read her Bible, Mother discovered some encouraging verses:

"Unto the upright there ariseth light in the darkness" (Ps. 112:4).

"The people that walked in darkness have seen a great light: they that dwell in the land of the shadow of death, upon them hath the light shined" (Isa. 9:2).

"He discovereth deep things out of darkness, and bringeth out to light the shadow of death" (Job 12:22).

Excitedly, Mother went to her pastor to share what God was teaching her.

"From what I've been reading in the Bible," she confided, "I think that Jesus Christ can take care of the problem I have in our home!"

"My dear woman," answered the pastor, "The Scriptures to which you are referring are not for you and me. They were for people living in Bible times."

"But I'm suffering!" Mother said as she wiped the tears away. "I don't know what to do! I can't cope with my husband; I'm too small and weak. He often gets drunk too. Pastor, what shall I do?"

"Leave him!" The pastor almost spit the words in disgust, as he crossed his legs and leaned back in his chair. "He's hopeless. You have every scriptural right to leave him. If you continue living with him, he'll ruin your family."

> God writes the Gospel not in the Bible alone, but also in the trees, and in the flowers, and clouds, and stars.
>
> MARTIN LUTHER

"Thank you for your time." Mother whispered. Stuffing her handkerchief in her pocket, she stumbled out the door and trudged home with a broken heart. "I can't leave him, Lord!" she cried. "That wouldn't be good for the children. But oh, please show me what to do!" Mother kept searching her Scriptures until one day she found another comforting verse:

> "Wherefore he is able also to save them to the uttermost that come unto God by him, seeing he ever liveth to make intercession for them" (Heb. 7:25).

> Nobody ever outgrows Scripture; the book widens and deepens with our years.
>
> **CHARLES SPURGEON**

In the Norwegian Bible, the verse is translated: "He is able also to cure them to the uttermost..." "Uttermost" means the "farthest point beyond the farthest point." She got so excited about this verse that she went back to her pastor.

"Pastor!" she exclaimed, "I've found the most wonderful scripture! God says he can cure my husband in spite of his awful condition. And he can help my children too!"

The pastor adjusted his glasses and glared at her. "Listen, Mrs. Iverson, I'm asking you to stop putting your own meaning to the Scriptures. Since you have had no training, you don't have the capacity to understand the Holy Scriptures." He measured every word. The wrinkles in his brow deepened. "I'm asking you to stop this practice of misinterpreting the Bible!"

But Mother couldn't stop. She kept seeking the Lord and searching the Bible. One day she found a verse that gave her the key to victory:

> "...and God saw everything that he had made, and, behold, it was very good." (Gen. 1:31).

"Why," Mother exclaimed, "God made my husband; He made my children. And He made them very good! I don't see them being good now, but if God says they're good, some day they will be!" Mother almost skipped along the rough country road to the parsonage to show this wonderful verse to her pastor. Instead of rejoicing with her, he scowled at her.

"Mrs. Iverson," he accused, with flushed face, "I can't stand your tormenting me with these strange interpretations. Now, please go and don't bother me again." Mother froze, too stunned to reply. It was as if her pastor had slapped her in the face. Then, picking up her Bible and purse with trembling fingers, she stumbled out of the room. Her heart felt like stone. What had she done that was so terrible? Why had her own pastor acted like that? Suddenly hot tears stung her eyes as she thought, "Where will I go to church now?" She neither spoke nor understood much English, and this was the only Norwegian church in the community. "Oh Lord! What am I going to do?" she cried in agony. Mother did the best thing she could do; every day she retreated to her bedroom and spent time with the Lord. She prayed, she read and searched the Scriptures. Then, perhaps to keep her mind from wandering, Mother began reading her Bible out loud. In so doing, she discovered one of the greatest concepts I know of—the power of affirmative declarations—the miracle of the mouth. As she read the first chapter of Genesis out loud, she suddenly realized that when God spoke, things happened. When He said, "Let there be light," there was light. Whatever He said came into being. Later she saw the same thought in Hebrews 11:3, "Through faith we understand that the worlds were framed by the word of God..." From the book of Revelation she learned that God is going to destroy the world by the words of his mouth (Rev. 19:15). Mother took off her apron and put on her old shoes and sweater. It was time to go out and hoe. She took a deep breath of the clear morning air as she closed the kitchen door behind her. The dew was clinging to the grass in the shimmering crystals.

The grinding work was still there, demanding to be done; her husband and her son still drank and cursed as much as ever. But somehow, after time spent with the Lord, and His Word, everything looked beautiful. Mother was changing.

"Dear God," she said as she moved the hoe deftly around the corn stalks, "I see now that Your words somehow make Your will and program happen. Now, Father, how can I use my words to see Your will done in my family?" In her simple reasoning, Mother began thinking that the mouth is the gateway to the stomach.

> We may ignore, but we can nowhere evade the presence of God. The world is crowded with Him. He walks everywhere incognito.
>
> C.S. LEWIS

"There must be a 'mouth' opening to the heart, too," she pondered. "Why, I see it now! The mind is the gateway to the heart!" One day she read a verse, which suddenly became very meaningful to her: "The Lord of hosts hath sworn, saying, Surely as I have thought, so shall it come to pass; and as I have purposed, so shall it stand" (Isa. 14:24).

"God thought, God said, and then what He said came to pass," Mother mused. Mother began to understand that if God worked this way, she could too.

Anna sought God's direction when dealing with the tribulations in her life. When the church failed to support her, she found guidance in her little black Norwegian Bible. Even as circumstances worsened in subsequent years, it was her little black Bible that inspired her to grow her relationship with God. As her relationship with God deepened, she became a vessel of many supernatural healings in her family. Today, she is widely regarded as the spiritual matriarch of the Iverson family. Anna's heart for God led to generations of Christian advocates within my family and is the reason why I have a passion for Christian spirituality myself. Just like it was for Anna, the Bible has been a transformative spiritual guide for my family.

For the first twenty years of my life, I read the Bible literally. I believed it was inerrant, each word coming from God's mouth directly. It was not until college that I learned that the Bible had, in fact, gone through numerous revisions, had numerous contradictions and historical inaccuracies, and was culturally biased. I remember wrestling with these realities, which ultimately led me to reject the Bible for a period of time. As the years passed, however, I began to accept these new understandings. I started to see that my past interpretation of the Bible had limited my relationship with God. I knew this because now, after accepting that the Bible was not the literal Word of God, God's presence became much greater within my life. The Bible is certainly inspired by God. Through reading it, many (including myself) have experienced spiritual transformation and a deepening of their relationship with God. The Bible can be a huge resource on the spiritual journey. Yet, for many Christians, the Bible has become an idol.

The Idolization of the Bible

Within most Protestant communities, the Bible is considered the medium between man and God. It is synonymous with the Word of God, and whenever one says "The Word of God" the Bible is the first image that comes to the Protestant's mind. As I hope you will see, the merging of the Bible with the Word of God is a dangerous conflation.

Before the Protestant Reformation, Christians relied solely on the church for spiritual guidance. The Bible, established by the church centuries after Jesus, was also used. Being written in Latin, however, only a few (primarily the clergy) were able to read the Bible. Common people had to trust the clergy to translate what was in the Biblical text as well as give their interpretation. This gave the clergy immense power. Over time the church became corrupted, implementing doctrines that were vastly opposite of Jesus's teachings. One such doctrine was the teaching of indulgences. Christians were taught that if they paid the church they would pay the penalty of their sins and God would forgive them. They could also pay off the sins of their deceased loved ones, guaranteeing them entrance into heaven. It was not

> God is a circle whose center is everywhere and circumference is nowhere.
>
> VOLTAIRE

until Martin Luther, an educated priest who could read Latin, compared the teachings in the Bible to current church practice and saw the extensive corruption. In response, Luther wrote and nailed his 95 Theses on the door of the Castle Church in Wittenberg, Germany. This initiated the Protestant Reformation, the first real collective questioning of the Catholic Church since the Great Schism (the divorce of the Catholic and Orthodox churches) of 1054 C.E. Five years later Luther translated the Bible into German, making it possible for the common person to read it. Thanks to Johannes Guttenberg's invention of the printing press, Bibles were mass produced and widely distributed. People all throughout Europe started to read the Bible for themselves, learning about the life and teachings of Jesus and the beginnings of Christianity and witnessed how far the church had strayed. They then battled within themselves whether or not to remain faithful to their long-held tradition or enter the religious unknown and risk accusations of heresy. Those that valued the teachings in the Bible over their affiliation with the church initiated a "New Age" Christianity, known today as Protestantism.

After leaving the Catholic Church, Protestants felt the need to find an authority to center their Christian faith and practice. They were quick to place this authority in the Bible. Afterall, it was the Bible that allowed Luther and other Christians to see the church's corruption in the first place. The reverence of the Bible grew and grew within

Protestant communities. From this arose a new doctrine known as *sola scriptura*, that is, the Bible became the sole authority of Christian faith and practice. With the emphasis of this doctrine, the Bible gained the spiritual elevation equivalent to the Pope. In doing so, it became considered the only Word of God.

Herein lies a major spiritual obstruction. The merging of the concept of the Word of God, which is dynamic and eternal, with the Bible, which is fixed and written by man, not only put God within the confines of a single book but it eliminated the possibility that God can still speak new revelations to people today. Who are we to limit God's revelations and who God decides to give revelations to? Are we more "God" than God? This merging suggests that God suddenly stopped speaking to people after the first century, for no real apparent reason. I remember being told as a child that God used to speak to people audibly in the Bible days but stopped speaking to people in modern times. We no longer have the same direct access to God as Abraham, Moses, Elijah, Isaiah, Jesus, Paul, and numerous others in the Bible had. God is somehow more distant to us now, which is strange because Jesus came to open our eyes and hearts to God. This new belief quickly led Protestants to forfeit their own possible God-experiences and put all reliance on the God-experience of those who went before them.

I would like to point out a verse that is commonly used to justify the theology of *sola scriptura*. The verse comes from the book of Revelation.

> *For I testify unto every man that heareth the words of the prophecy of this book, if any man shall add unto these things, God shall add unto him the plagues that are written in this book:*
> *And if any man shall take away from the words of the book of this prophecy, God shall take away his part out of the book of life, and out of the holy city, and from the things which are written in this book.*
> (Revelation 22:18-19)

I have heard Protestant Christians apply this passage of scripture to the entire Bible. This is likely because the verse mentions "this book," which some assume to be the Bible. Yet, canonization of the Bible came hundreds of years after the recording of Revelation. It is thus inaccurate to assume

> Listen to God's voice in everything you do and everywhere you go; He's the one that will keep you on track.
>
> **PROVERBS 3:6**

that John was talking about the Bible. In fact, it is a pretty far stretch to assume that any author in the Bible believed their writings would become revered scriptures.

What is clear is this: the Bible is inspired. It has been the source of numerous healings and transformations. It has provided comfort to millions of Christians for thousands of years. It is the book that helped give my great-grandma faith and courage. It is the book that transformed my grandpa's life from a life of wretchedness to a life of love. It is the book that gave me inspiration to continuously seek God. The Bible is certainly a Word of God, but it is not *the* Word of God. The Bible can be the jumping off point, but it is not the endpoint. It is not the Bible itself that brings one closer to God; rather, it is the movement within the soul through the reading of the Bible that brings one closer to God. We worship the God of the Bible, but we must be careful not to worship the Bible as God. Be aware of this idolatry.

If the Word of God is eternal, then it is silly to assume the Word of God is the Bible, since the Bible has only been around for a couple thousand years. As Jesus said:

> *You search the scriptures because you think that in them you have eternal life; it is these that testify about me; and you are unwilling to come to me so that you may have life." (John 5:39-40)*

The Bible points to the Way, but it is not the Way itself. Jesus is the Way. So if the Word of God is not the Bible, then what is the Word of God?

The Word Beyond the Text

Let us take a look at the famous mystical lines of the Gospel of John.

> *In the beginning was the Word, and the Word was with God, and the Word was God. He was with God in the beginning. Through him all things were made; without him nothing was made that has been made. In him was life, and that life was the light of all mankind. The light shines in the darkness, and the darkness has not overcome it.* (John 1:1-5)

The Word of God is God's expression through creation. All things were made by the Word of God. It is the Word of God which created the world. The Word said, "Let there be light," and the physical world came into existence. The Word of God is God manifested. This is why the Word of God is often associated with Jesus, who Christians claim is the manifestation of God on earth. Yet, God has been manifesting Godself since the beginning of time. God was certainly manifesting Godself before the invention of writing. It was not until the rise of civilization and the development of languages that the Word of God became manifested in writing. The Word of God, therefore, cannot be limited to a book.

The Word of God is dynamic. The Word of God is the same yesterday, today, and forever. The Word of God is ever-revealing, ever-manifesting. The Word of God certainly spoke through the various authors of the Bible. The Word of God flowed through these authors who wrote their revelations in their own languages, using their own writing styles, within their own cultural understanding, and carrying their own biases. The Bible certainly is a vessel of the Word of God. As the Apostle Paul told his disciple, Timothy:

All scripture is God-breathed and is useful for teaching, rebuking, correcting and training in righteousness, so that the servant of God may be thoroughly equipped for every good work. (2 Timothy 3:16-17)

I am with you always
even to the end
of the world.

MATTHEW 28:20

Paul did not say that scripture was God's only Word. Paul said that all scripture is *breathed* by the Word of God.

We must be able to distinguish between the written text and the Word of God which speaks through the written text. To help differentiate between the Word of God and the text, the reader can ask themselves the following questions:

Who wrote this book and for what audience?

What is the historical context of this book?

How did cultural understandings influence the book's writing?

What biases did the author have? How did the author's bias influence the book's writing?

What is the author's underlying spiritual message?

Anybody can read the Bible. It does not mean the reader will always come to know God. Atheists read the Bible and reject the existence of God. It is not the reading of the Bible that brings one closer to God; it is opening oneself to the Word of God as one reads the Bible and allowing the Word to reveal itself. It takes an open seeker, unattached to the Bible, to see the Word that lies within the Bible. Once the Word is identified, the individual will see the Word expressed over and over again through the Biblical text. No matter the historical inaccuracies, no matter the contradictions, no matter the biases, when guided by the Word, the Bible becomes a powerful spiritual tool.

This leads to the next question: if the Word of God is different from the Bible, then can God speak to us outside the Bible? This we will look at next.

The Word Expressed through Different Mediums

Imagine you are a student in high school and are given a writing assignment. Perhaps you are assigned a topic you aren't too interested in. As you may discover through the writing process, ideas and words may be difficult to come by. You likely will struggle to write a masterpiece, and your finished product will probably feel inadequate. On the other hand, maybe the topic you are given interests you. As you go through the writing process, ideas and words may flow out of you like a torrent, as if there was a deeper force writing the words for you. You may even find it difficult for your hand to keep up with your mental outpouring! This is what inspiration means: to be *in-spirited*, or allowing a deeper spirit to speak from within you. As a musician, my best songs came out of a place of inspiration, where the words and melody flowed out of me without much mental effort. On the other hand, I remember there were times when I tried to force myself to write a song and it turned out terrible. An artist's best work, a musician's best songs, and an author's best book arise from a space of total receptivity of a greater internal force.

This is how the Word of God operates; from a place of *in-spiration*. The Word of God is not limited to any one particular medium of expression. The Word of God is much bigger than that. The Word of God can speak through the Bible, but the Word of God is not limited to the Bible. Even the great Protestant pioneer Martin Luther once said:

> God writes the Gospel not in the Bible alone, but also in the trees, and in the flowers, and clouds, and stars.

The Word of God may speak to you while you are weeding your garden. The Word of God may speak to you while viewing a beautiful art piece. The Word of God may speak to you while reading an uplifting book. The Word of God may speak to you

> God is everywhere. You decide whether you are close to Him or not.
>
> JOHN CHRYSOSTOM

when observing the surrounding mountains and the rivers that flow from them. The Word of God may speak to you when hearing a baby laughing. The Word of God may speak to you while passing a homeless man or woman on the street. The Word of God may speak to you when playing an inspiring tune. The Word of God is multifaceted, dynamic and continuous.

Inspired texts, spiritual communities, creative expression and reception, dreams and visions, nature, wisdom, intuition, dark night experiences, contemplative prayer, and peak experiences can all be mediums for the Word of God. In no way is this list complete (I am sure I missed some medium!). Be that as it may, I have condensed all mediums into ten general categories. Let us take a brief look at each.

1. **Inspired texts**. Scriptures possess immense spiritual power. For generations people have been influenced, transformed and spoken to by the Word through the reading of scriptures. The Bible is the prime example, as it has been a channel of the Word of God for Christians for thousands of years and remains a channel today. The Bible is surely the greatest resource for learning about the life and teachings of Jesus. But the Bible is not the only spiritual text worth investigating. Besides the Christian scriptures, there are other scriptures worth

reading that are considered sacred to spiritual seekers of the other world religions (ex. the Quran, Bhagavad Gita, Dhammapada). To further add, there are other inspired texts that are not institutionally canonized from both the past and the present that can inspire souls to open their hearts to the Divine. Do not be afraid to read a book that is calling you just because some other book condemned it.

2. **Spiritual communities**. When two or more people gather together and focus on the Divine, there is a real possibility of a direct God encounter (Matthew 18:20). Whether you identify yourself as a Christian, a Jew, a Muslim, a Buddhist, a Hindu, an atheist or a New Age practitioner, any gathering that is focused on spiritual development is sure to grow your relationship with God. Being part of a spiritually-focused community may be the key to opening oneself to the Divine Word. More will be described in the ninth chapter of this book.

3. **Creative expression and reception.** We are created in the image of God and as God is our Creator, we are likewise creators. When we are in alignment with our creative energy, we are allowing God's very self to shine through us in unique ways. By creating, we are ultimately giving God the glory. Creation is the art of surrendering to *in-spiration*, the internal Word that does the creating for you. You are simply the vessel of the Word, allowing it to penetrate your human vessel made up of mind, emotions, and sensations. Creation is known to occur through the fine arts of music, architecture, poetry, sculpture and painting, but it can also occur through simple mundane tasks such

as reorganizing the furniture in the home, finding the best location to plant a tree, or daring to veer from the recipe of a certain meal. One can also receive the Word through the creation of another. Some of the greatest spiritual experiences I have had in my life have been going to concerts. When I stand in front of a band and hear certain sound combinations (such as vibrato in lead vocals or the deep bass projected through the subwoofers), it is as if my soul melts into the sound, bringing me into a deeper state of vibration. People have the same experience when looking at a particular art piece or watching a moving scene in a film. Unlike scriptures, which are relatively fixed in revelation, artistic expression and reception allows the individual to experience new revelations. Do not be fooled that God's revelations somehow ceased 2000 years ago. Jesus did not come to end divine revelation. Rather, Jesus tore the veil between this world and heaven and opened the possibility for people to experience the Word here and now through whatever medium available.

4. **Dreams and visions**. Some of the more powerful mystical experiences have come in the forms of dreams and visions. God spoke to numerous characters in the Bible through dreams and visions. God spoke to Joseph through dreams (Genesis 37:1-11). God told Abraham in a vision that he would be a father of many nations (Genesis 15:1). Jacob dreamt of a ladder

> God is everywhere and in everything and without Him we cannot exist.
>
> MOTHER TERESA

reaching to heaven where angels ascended and descended (Genesis 28:10-11). Samuel, Solomon, Daniel, Zacharias, Joseph (Mary's husband), Pilate's wife, Peter, Paul, John the Revelator, and countless others had dreams or visions which changed their life trajectory. God can likewise speak to you through dreams and visions.

5. **Nature**. Before the Bible existed, nature *was*. As pastor and author Max Lucado said, "Nature is God's first missionary. Where there is no Bible there are sparkling stars. Where there are not preachers there are spring times…If a person has nothing but nature, then nature is enough to reveal something about God." Throughout history people have turned to nature to discover God. Many spiritual initiation ceremonies involve going out into nature to connect with the Divine. Nature is certainly a medium of the Word.

6. **Wisdom**. American writer, historian, and philosopher Will Durant once said, "Knowledge is power but only wisdom is liberty." Wisdom includes but is not confined to knowledge. Knowledge may be helpful in holding to a truth but it can also prove ineffective when discerning truth during a novel situation, as the mind may have little time to evaluate. Wisdom, on the other hand, is the ability to perceive truth in the moment. As all truth stems from God, all wisdom also stems from God as the Word. Solomon is described as a man of wisdom. In one famous Biblical story, he used his wisdom to discern which of two women claiming to be a baby's mother was the real mother (1 Kings 3:16-28). He had no DNA tests to make his final judgment. Instead, he used his wisdom to guide him in

making the correct decision. The Word as wisdom helps us to eliminate falsities and discern truth. The Word as wisdom can see both the light and the shadow.

7. **Intuition.** Intuition, like wisdom, is an inner knowing of truth in the moment. Unlike wisdom which is thought-dominant, intuition is feeling-dominant. Let me give you a couple examples. If you go to the park and have a bad feeling leaving your child unattended, it is probably your intuition speaking. Similarly, if you get the feeling to pass on a certain business deal even though all reasoning tells you to make the deal, your intuition is probably speaking to you. Most of us have been taught to ignore our intuition in favor of reasoning. This is unfortunate, because the Word may be speaking to you through your intuition to help you make the best decision. You have probably experienced making a bad decision in your life based on reasoning and ignoring your intuition, to later realize your intuition was right all along. When your intuition is telling you something, it is best to listen.

8. **Dark night experiences.** It often takes suffering to shake us from our egoic attachments. As the Buddha said, "The root of suffering is attachment." It is always difficult when something challenges our established

> The Bible is there to enable God's people to be equipped to do God's work in God's world, not to give them an excuse to sit back smugly, knowing they possess all God's truth.
>
> NT WRIGHT

perceptions. Our perceptions are the foundation of our identity. If we have a great life, we have little desire to lose this identity and will do whatever we can to hold onto it. This is attachment. Dark night experiences are a sure way to loosen the grips of our perceived identities and allow an opening for divine revelation. The symbolism of the death of Jesus and the resurrection of Christ speaks of our own suffering and the death of the self in order to be fully "born-again." These dark night experiences suck, no doubt. Transitioning to a relationship-centered spirituality is not supposed to be easy. Yet, for some strange reason the dark night experiences work to shift our consciousness to the deeper truths only found in God, and thus our only relief is to turn to that relationship alone. Then our vessels are cleared for the Word to speak. One question we can reflect upon to help us during a dark night experience: what does it mean to "take up our cross" and follow Christ?

9. **Contemplative prayer.** What can also be referred to as meditation or simply prayer, contemplation is the act of silencing the world around us (including our own thoughts, emotions, and sensations) and focusing on our inner connection with God. St. Teresa of Avila said it best: "Contemplative prayer in my opinion is nothing else than a close sharing between friends; it means taking time frequently to be alone with [God] who we know loves us." In silencing the chaos of both the inner and the outer worlds, contemplative prayer opens our vessels for the Word to speak to us.

10. **Peak experiences**. Intense encounters with the Divine
    can occur as a peak experience. Peak experiences, or
    mystical experiences, are experiences that alter a person's
    consciousness. American psychologist Abraham Maslow
    coined the term and described the experiences to be
    "rare, exciting, organic, deeply moving, exhilarating,
    elevating experiences that generate an advanced form
    of perceiving reality, and are even mystical and magical
    in their effect upon the experimenter." Peak experiences
    can come in the forms of near-death experiences (NDEs),
    psychedelic experiences, tranced experiences, meditation
    experiences, or they can occur randomly. Peak experiences
    are infrequent, however they do occur. Most people who
    have had peak experiences speak of encountering a reality
    that is more real than this world. The Word has certainly
    worked through peak experiences.

As Christians who seek to be led by the Word of God, we must detach from our idolization of any one particular medium of the Word of God, for God may be speaking to us in a multitude of ways. If you have a desire to know God directly rather than relying on second-hand knowledge, if you desire to be a vessel of the Word of God yourself, you must remain open to the Word's revelation whenever and wherever it presents itself. God's revelation is ongoing, and it is being spoken to you now. Can you hear it?

Then he opened their minds to understand the scriptures. (Luke 24:45)

Reflection Questions

1. What spiritual impact has the Bible had on my life?

_____

_____

_____

2. How can I identify the Word within the Bible?

_____

_____

_____

3. If I did not have a Bible, how would I hear from God?

_____

_____

_____

4. How have I personally experienced the Word of God outside of the Bible?

_____

_____

_____

Prayer Practice

To enable the Word of God to speak through the Bible, any Bible reading must be accompanied by prayer. As you read the Bible, use the following strategy.

1. **Set a spiritual intention.** To grow your relationship with God, you must approach the Bible from a spiritual mindset. Set an intention for opening yourself to hear from and receive from the Word of God.

2. **Free yourself from a literal interpretation.** It is ineffective and dangerous reading the Bible from a mere literal point of view. The authors of the Bible lived in a different era, within a different culture, and had different beliefs, many of which are outdated. I mean, do we really want to recreate a culture that encourages the pillaging of towns and the eradication of every man, woman, child and animal? Would it be wise to bring back animal sacrifice to make amends to an archaic God? Do we really want to reestablish a patriarchal society where women are seen and treated as subordinates? Is it really necessary to bring back

the culture of martyrdom? Are any of these necessary to know God? The spiritual messages in the Biblical text are beneath the literal.

3. **Understand the context of what you are reading.** Who wrote it? For what audience? What was the author's culture? What was the surrounding geography like? What are the author's biases? What are the cultures and influences around? Why did the author write this book? What was their main message? Asking these types of questions creates space and movement within the text, from which point you move on to step four.

4. **Pray and ask God to give you spiritual insight.** How does this passage connect to spirituality? Delve into your prayer practice. Meditate on the passage you read. Let the passage sink in. Let it transform your consciousness. Let the Word speak to you, if the Word wills it. Ending with the Word is the whole point.

9

From Building to Assembly:

How We View Church

IN 2010 MY FAMILY and I started attending a new local church. We had first heard about this church through a flyer we received in the mail. We had been frequently going to a small Assembly of God church some distance away and were longing for a home church that was closer so we could be more involved. When we stepped through the foyer doors of that new church that first Sunday morning it felt like we were walking into a megachurch. As we entered the main sanctuary, we noticed a widespread stage with a brand new sound system. There were a couple keyboards, several guitars, a bass, a drum set with a shield, and bongo drums. Obviously money was invested in music ministry, which made us really excited since we were musicians. Off the stage we noticed hundreds of chairs, many more than we were used to in the church we had previously attended. I could not believe our small hometown could accommodate a church like this! We were excited to join this new and growing Christian community.

We attended the new church for three years. We met with the pastor and his wife rather quickly, and before long we did a "try out" for the worship team. We felt pretty confident going into the tryouts. As we went on stage we did a few contemporary songs that we thought would be familiar, as well as some of our own originals. We felt we were being critiqued like on American Idol! After we completed our set, the pastor came up on stage and told us that we had made the worship team. We were excited to be accepted by the pastor and the church leaders, and marveled at the opportunity to serve in the music ministry at the church.

Once a week we came into the church to practice with the worship team. I was asked to play the keyboard and fill in with vocals, and my siblings and mother were given vocal roles as well. We accepted these roles, for we knew a quality worship team required all the parts working in harmony. The worship leader was the pastor's wife (who was also the co-pastor), and we came to discover that she was quite territorial. I remember one time when she forgot the words to a song that my mother jumped in and sang the verse through. The pastor's wife then snapped at her saying, "That's my part!" After that experience, my mother was never invited back up to sing. This was the start of a series of red flags.

The pastor was quite dictatorial as well. Every Sunday after preaching his sermon, I remember the pastor would call up the worship team to close out the service. As we played he would give his closing prayer and remarks. After dismissing the congregation, the pastor quickly got off the stage, put his head down avoiding all interaction, and walked straight out the back door and disappeared into his office. He never said a word to anybody, something I had never experienced in a pastor before. This was red flag number two.

> Our relationship with each other is the criterion the world uses to judge whether our message is truthful. Christian community is the final apologetic.
>
> **FRANCIS SCHAEFFER**

As time went on the church began to struggle financially. The pastor came to the conclusion that members of the church were not giving enough in tithes, and the only way to balance the budgets was that members needed to give more and/or new members needed to be added. As members of the worship team, we were then required to become members of the church. I had never

> The church is not the building, it's the people; it's not just the gathering, it's also the scattering.
>
> JOHN WIMBER

been a member of a church before. Nevertheless, I enjoyed being involved with music ministry so I decided to meet the pastor's call. To become a member, we had to go through a program called "Discipleship Training School," created by the pastor himself. For several Sunday mornings we met with the pastor in the side room as he trained us in his theology. I remember him telling us once that the church is not a democracy, that there is indeed a hierarchy of power. This was strange to me, as I always assumed church was more democratic. To me this church felt more like a dictatorship. Regardless, I ignored my intuition and finished the program. At the end of Discipleship Training School, we signed a form that committed ourselves to membership and supporting the church in tithing, talent, and time.

Time went on, and things got even weirder. We knew the pastors were stressed about finances, as the church struggled to attract new members. It was shocking, however, to witness the corruption behind the scenes of the church. I began to see this corruption through a series of actions. First, the pastor took great pride in his luxuries. I remember he had posted a picture of his brand new fancy red car on Facebook. This came shortly after his sermon shaming his church congregation for not giving enough in tithes. I wondered: for a church that is struggling so much financially, how is this man able to afford this car? This was certainly different than selling one's possessions and giving to the poor as Jesus taught (Luke 18:22). Second, I found it strange when the pastor instructed us to take out a third of the chairs in the sanctuary to make it look like the attendance numbers were higher than they actually were. Obviously, the pastor valued appearances. His passion for keeping up appearances was a little overwhelming, and it seemed to radiate stronger than his passion for God. Third, during a team meeting the pastor and his wife told us that they were going to start tracking our tithing. Why would the pastor and his wife feel the need to track our tithing? It felt like we were not trusted. This action would also most certainly lead to future condemnation for those who did not give.

At home that evening, my family and I discussed the red flags and decided to renounce our membership from the church. We knew that this would probably boot us off the worship team, but we felt we had to make this decision. That night we wrote a letter to the pastors formally renouncing our membership. We received no reply back. Days later, we noticed the lead pastor deleted all of us from his Facebook, the last contact we ever made with him. It felt like a true excommunication. That was the last church we faithfully attended.

The Evolution of God's House

For years I believed that the church was where one went to find God. You could certainly experience God outside the church, but if you truly wanted to grow your relationship with God you needed to attend a church. Years later I discovered that a lot of what I experienced in church was superfluous and far from the original meaning of church.

In the ancient world deities were believed to have been located in specific places. These locations were most often called temples or shrines. Whether you lived in Mesopotamia, the Near East, Egypt, Greece, or the Americas, temples were erected as the biggest, boldest, and the most holy building within the city where the deities could be found. At these temples people sacrificed to the deities and prayed for prosperity, health, and protection. Worshippers believed that by sacrificing to the deities, the deities would bless them in return. The practices in ancient Israel and Judah were no exception.

> May every Church and Christian community be a place of mercy amid so much indifference.
>
> **POPE FRANCIS**

In the book of Exodus, the tabernacle was described as the first dwelling place of their god, Yahweh. Also called the Tent of the Congregation, the tabernacle was mobile, carried by the Hebrews from place to place as they wandered the desert. It was here that the Ark of the Covenant, a gold-covered wooden chest containing Moses' two stone tablets, Aaron's rod, and a golden pot with manna, was placed. The Ark of the Covenant was believed to hold the actual presence of Yahweh. It was so holy, it is said, that if you even touched it Yahweh would strike you dead.

After the Hebrews established permanent locations in Canaan, temples began to replace the tabernacle as the dwelling place of God. Solomon's Temple is the most famous of these temples. It is believed to have been the resting place of the Ark of the Covenant. Although archaeologists have yet to discover evidence of Solomon's Temple, they have uncovered various temples throughout the lands of the Near East that were erected to the god Yahweh. Just like other surrounding nations, the Hebrews made sacrifices to Yahweh in these various temples. During these times there were some who believed that God's presence extended beyond the temple, although this appears to be a rarity. King David was one of these individuals, who believed in God's omnipresence.

Where can I go from Your Spirit?
Or where can I flee from Your presence?
If I ascend to heaven, You are there;
If I make my bed in Sheol, behold, You are there.
If I take the wings of the dawn,
If I dwell in the remotest part of the sea,
Even there Your hand will lead me,
And Your right hand will lay hold of me.
If I say, "Surely the darkness will overwhelm me,
And the light around me will be night,"
Even the darkness is not dark to You,
And the night is as bright as the day.
Darkness and light are alike to You. (Psalm 139:7-12)

David's son, Solomon, who built the first national temple of Israel, likewise admitted that no temple could contain the omnipresent God:

But will God really dwell on earth? The heavens, even the highest
heaven, cannot contain you. How much less this temple I have built!
(1 Kings 8:27)

Centuries later Jesus taught that the temple would be destroyed. This immediately created a division between Jesus and the religious leaders of his day. After all, the religious leaders believed the temple was the dwelling place of God. After his death, Jesus' disciples shifted their focus from the temple to the "church". Unlike the temple and the tabernacle before it, the church was not a building but rather a community of followers of Jesus.

> One of the marvelous
> things about community
> is that it enables us
> to welcome and help
> people in a way we
> couldn't as individuals.
>
> JEAN VANIER

Beyond a Building

If I asked the question, "What is church?" what would be your initial thoughts? For many Christians, church is like the temple: a physical place where like-minded Christians gather to worship God. The Merriam-Webster dictionary further jus-

> We cannot live only for ourselves. A thousand fibers connect us with our fellow men.
>
> HERMAN MELVILLE

tifies this understanding in its definition of church as "a building for public and Christian worship." Christians are continuously being guided to find a church home, and encouraged to stay faithful to that church so that they may grow in their faith. Over the years I have come to realize the stigma attached to the non-churchgoer. Any Christian that is not a member of a church or does not attend a church regularly is seen as less credible in spiritual matters in the eyes of churchgoing members.

One can see the reasoning why church leaders emphasize the need to attend weekly church services. Like the religious leaders in Jesus' day, church leaders depend on the faithfulness of their congregations. It is common to find church leaders focus their message on bringing more people into the church and stressing tithing. Unfortunately for many of these churches, bringing more people into the church holds greater importance than building the people spiritually who are already in the church. As I hope to show in this chapter, this is a far cry from the church's original purpose.

The word "church" is translated from the Greek word *ekklesia*. *Ek* means "out from" or "out to" and *kaleo* means "to call." *Ekklesia* can be translated as an assembly of those called out or an assembly summoned for a specific purpose. In ancient Greece, an *ekklesia* was an assembly of male citizens that got together in the city's agora, or outdoor public space, to discuss and make decisions about political matters such as assessing military strategy, electing leaders, and declaring war. Christians

> Alone, we can do so little; together, we can do so much.
>
> HELEN KELLER

adopted the concept of *ekklesia* and modified it to mean a group of Christians who assemble together.

The earliest Christians did not have church buildings. They did not have large sanctuaries with elevated pulpits and stages. They did not separate the priests from the lay people. They did not stress liturgies or doctrines. Rather, the first Christians assembled in each other's homes (Acts 17:5, 20:20; 1 Corinthians 16:19). This assembly supported each other spiritually, emotionally, and financially. The first tithes were not used to build church infrastructure or pay the church leaders. Rather, the first Christians used their tithes to help one another out. If one Christian was struggling in some way the assembly would support them. Community was of greatest importance, similar to the practices of our Paleolithic ancestors. It was in community that a Christian was able to practice what they preached, loving as Jesus loved. It was in community where one could go to express themselves and be understood. It was in community where one could be comforted.

The church is not a building where one goes to find God but rather an assembly of Christians who are already aware of God's presence within themselves. As Jesus told the Pharisees:

> *Neither shall they say, Lo here! Or, lo there! For, behold, the kingdom of God is within you. (Luke 17:21)*

Once we are aware that God is not in the temples of man but within our very hearts, we are sure to summon God's spirit should we assemble with other likeminded individuals. As Jesus said:

> *For where two or three gather in my name, there am I with them."* (Matthew 18:20)

When two or more are gathered together in Jesus' name, there arises a collective spiritual energy which expands the eternal presence of God within all individuals present. This is how *ekklesia* is to be an example to the rest of the world.

> If you want to go quickly, go alone. If you want to go far, go together.
>
> **AFRICAN PROVERB**

You are the light of the world. A town built on a hill cannot be hidden. (Matthew 5:14)

Jesus did not call for a centralized church or give an institutional requirement to know God. Rather, Jesus taught the importance of gathering together in spiritual intimacy.

Those of you who go to traditional churches, I encourage you to keep going if this is where you feel spiritually intimate. We need to support the ministries that stress relationships. Those who don't attend a traditional church, I encourage you to find a way to be in assembly with other spiritually-minded individuals. This does not have to be in a traditional church setting. It could be in your own home, as the early Christians did. It can be anywhere people are present and seeking God. It could be a dialogue with someone on a plane. It could be with your immediate family while eating dinner. It could be when you are on a hike with friends or playing on a sports team. You do not need to join an established church to have *ekklesia*. You *are* the church.

Remember: Christ is within you always, no matter your location.

> There is no power for change greater than a community discovering what it cares about.
>
> **MARGARET WHEATLEY**

I am with you always, even to the end of the world. (Matthew 28:20)

Reflection Questions

1. When I hear the word "church," what are the first words or images that come to mind?

_____

_____

_____

_____

_____

2. What are my experiences with the traditional church?

_____

_____

_____

_____

_____

3. What are my current views towards the church? How have my views changed over time?

_____

_____

_____

_____

_____

4. Do I currently go to church? How has this church impacted me spiritually?

_____

_____

_____

_____

_____

5. If I do not attend a church, what would the potential benefits be of joining a spiritual community?

_____

_____

_____

_____

_____

Prayer Practice

Consider assembling a group of spiritually-minded individuals. You only need two (or more) people. As you assemble, I advise having some form of spiritual text. This helps keep the assembly focused on spiritual matters versus becoming a mere social event. The text could be something in the Bible, in the Bhagavad Gita, in the Quran, or in another spiritual book. Do not fear studying the texts of various spiritual traditions. Studying other spiritual traditions will only enhance your understanding of God, trust me. I encourage you, as the assembly's facilitator, to come up with a topic and a series of discussion questions about the topic ahead of time. It is advisable to have some structure to the assembly as well. The following structure is one I recommend:

1. Begin by saying a prayer. You can do this yourself or have another volunteer give the prayer.

2. Read the spiritual passage together. Then give the topic and reflection questions to other assembly participants.

3. For the next 15-30 minutes, dedicate time to connecting with God individually. I like to turn on some meditation music, but you can do this in silence as well. The goal of this time is to contemplate a chosen passage and allow the Spirit to reveal itself. Towards the end of this time, I advise making a sound from something like a meditation bowl, cymbal, or gong so participants are not startled by a sudden stoppage. I would make this sound one minute before the ending of the prayer/meditation and once again at the very end. I would also let participants know ahead of time to listen out for this sound so they are not surprised.

4. Reassemble together. Give participants five minutes to answer the reflection questions. Then discuss these questions together, and allow each person to share what the Spirit revealed.

5. End with a prayer. Again, you can do this yourself or you can have another volunteer give the prayer.

10

From Conversion to Awakening:

How We View the Great Commission

WHEN I WAS A YOUNG TEENAGER I carried with me a strong sense of spiritual superiority. It was not because I was more spiritual; it was because I considered my religion to be superior to all others, especially my particular doctrines. Those who had different beliefs than me I saw as farther from God. As I would discover in later years, what I considered spiritual superiority was actually religious egotism.

When my older brother went to college he learned about spiritual traditions different from our childhood religion. I remember one weekend when he came home he started to describe to me different Eastern philosophies; concepts I had never even heard before. He came to the conclusion that all religions were connected at the mystical level. I immediately was sent into a state of anger. I thought: how could my brother fall away from God? My next reaction was fear. I didn't want my brother to burn in hell. Little did I expect that years later I would come to the same conclusion of a common trans-religious mysticism.

When I went to college myself I learned that Christianity was much more diverse and inclusionary than I previously knew. This gave me an immense security to explore a wide range of Christian beliefs. In the process, I became more tolerant of other pathways to God.

In 2008 I did my first study-abroad trip to Spain. Our focus during the trip was a study of the lives of the great Spanish mystics, notably St. Teresa of Avila and St. John of the Cross. I was fascinated by both their focuses on inner contemplation and union with God. I discovered in these two spiritual giants an inner spirituality that I always knew existed but had never come to fully know in my religious tradition. When I came home from Spain I went to my brother and told him about St. Teresa of Avila and St. John of the Cross. Surprisingly, he told me that he already knew who they were and studied them himself! How is it that my brother, who veered onto another spiritual path, also connected with the Spanish Christian mystics? From that point forward I realized there was something real and profound about the mystics, and I longed to dig further into that tradition.

In 2010 I experienced my greatest spiritual breakthrough. After going through a period of extensive suffering, I came to a place where I had to let go of all attachments of who I thought I was in order for my suffering to cease. This release caused me to die to my former self, leading me into the "Dark Night of the Soul". It was here that I came to experience a cosmic shift in my consciousness. Religion was no longer sufficient for me, for I saw man's great influence in it. It was the Christian mystics that kept me interested in Christianity, for I felt their descriptions of the spiritual world were my own. I began to also open myself to the studies of the mystics of other religious traditions too. I studied the likes of Rumi (the Sufi mystic), Ramana Maharshi (the Indian

> We can learn a lot from crayons; some are sharp, some are pretty, some are dull, while others are bright, some have weird names, but they all have learned to live together in the same box.
>
> ROBERT FULGHUM

mystic), and the Buddha. I saw commonalities in all mystical traditions- mainly the emphasis of going inward to know God. As Christian mystic Meister Eckhart accurately described:

> *Theologians may quarrel, but the mystics of the world speak the same language.*

Through the mystics I understood that religious union was possible.

What is the Great Commission?

Before his ascension to heaven, Jesus gave his disciples one last commandment. As Matthew records in his gospel:

> *Then the eleven disciples went to Galilee, to the mountain where Jesus had told them to go. When they saw him, they worshiped him; but some doubted. Then Jesus came to them and said, "All authority in heaven and on earth has been given to me. Therefore go and make disciples of all nations, baptizing them in the name of the Father and of the Son and of the Holy Spirit, and teaching them to obey everything I have commanded you. And surely I am with you always, to the very end of the age." (Matthew 28:16-20)*

The Great Commission, according to the beliefs of many Christians, is to make more Christians. Yet, Christianity did not exist at the time when Jesus said these words. So what was Jesus talking about? To answer that question, I think it would help us to go through the religious development of the Judeo-Christian heritage.

> Of all religions, the Christian should of course inspire the most tolerance, but until now Christians have been the most intolerant of all men.
>
> VOLTAIRE

The Evolution of Christian Spirituality

Throughout most of its history, Christianity has promoted a separatist perspective of other people and other religions. The fear of others and their beliefs have created very intolerant, egocentric Christians who believe it dangerous to explore other faith traditions. The origins of this separatist perspective go back to the ancient Hebrews, who intended to preserve the purity of their Jewish heritage within the context of an ever-changing mixture of cultures and spiritualties of the ancient Near East. As can clearly be seen through the readings of the Old Testament, the Jewish Scriptures promoted segregation from other cultures, and their kingdoms established many anti-miscegenation laws (laws meant to prevent interbreeding between people of different cultures or races) that would come to have long-term effects on future societies. With Judaism as its ancestor, Christianity adopted this drive of separation, and it still radiates strongly in Christianity to this day. As I hope to communicate in this chapter, neither Judaism nor Christianity have truly been religiously homogeneous and have a rather long history of inclusion of other cultures.

God never changes, but cultures, governments, and religions do. Many of the religious understandings Judeo-Christians once deemed absolute are now debated (such as the doctrine of purgatory) or have been completely discarded altogether (such as human and/or animal sacrifice). Likewise, many of the religious understandings we hold true today were not always true and will someday become obsolete as time passes. This reality should not freak us out; it should open our hearts and minds.

> All religions must be tolerated...for every man must get to heaven in his own way.
>
> EPICTETUS

Looking back at Jewish and Christian history, we can see a continuous story of the movement of people and the contributions of cultures to the Judeo-Christian identity. As I hope to present, Christians have been blending with and adopt-

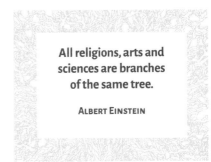

All religions, arts and sciences are branches of the same tree.

ALBERT EINSTEIN

ing from other cultures and religions all along. I think it is essential for the Christian to study the roots of their religion and become aware of its evolution over time. This ought to make us question our own arrogance and attachment to Christianity as a religion. By doing so perhaps the Christian will begin to see that the call of the Great Commission was not to make more Christians (again, there was no Christianity at the time that Jesus gave this commandment) but was instead meant to awaken the hearts and minds of individuals from all religious traditions. Jesus's call went beyond any one religion.

Let me present you with a brief history of the evolution of Christianity, starting from its earliest Canaanite roots in polytheism and ending in the postmodern world of globalization. All the information below was unearthed through my own studies. Do your own research to verify what I have to present (and don't just read from Christian sources!).

Canaanite Polytheism (1200-930 BCE)

Archaeological evidence suggests that the Israelites did not conquer Canaan by force, as described in the book of Joshua. Instead, according to archaeologists, the Israelites emerged out of the various indigenous Canaanite peoples that were already inhabiting the area of Canaan. The Canaanites were polytheistic and worshiped many gods. Some of these gods included El, Baal, Asherah, Dagon, Chemosh, Moloch, and Mot. El was the supreme god of the Canaanite pantheon. El (also known as El Shaddai, El Elyon, Eloah, or Elohim) appears 217 times in the Old Testament, primarily in the books of Psalms and Job. El was probably the god of Abraham, Isaac, and Jacob. The very name *Israel* comes from the word El (*El contended* or *wrestling with El*). The Islamic name for God, Allah, is also descended from the name El. El in his earliest form had a consort named Asherah, also known as the Mother Goddess.

The origins of Yahweh are a little vague. Although historians believe the Hebrews were Canaanites, Yahweh was not of Canaanite origin. Sadly, the original meaning of Yahweh has been lost in time. The oldest record of Yahweh's name was discovered in an Egyptian inscription from the time of Amenhotep III describing the land of the Shasu people. The Shasu were cattle nomads who worshiped the god Yahu (Yhw), what scholars believe to be proto-Yahweh. Another interesting fact was that the Shasu people lived in Midian, the same place Moses encountered God in the burning bush. Some historians believe that through the caravans of the Shasu people between Egypt and Canaan, Yahweh eventually found himself in the land of Canaan. Groups of displaced Canaanites clung to this new god Yahweh, differentiating themselves as Hebrews amongst the numerous surrounding Canaanite tribes. The Hebrews would come to establish the kingdoms of Israel and Judah. Besides Yahweh, the Hebrews continued to worship the Canaanite gods.

Over time, El merged with Yahweh. El became the generic name for god, while Yahweh became the supreme god of the Hebrews. Yahweh headed the Hebrew pantheon of lesser Canaanite gods along with his consort, Asherah (an obvious adoption from El). Other Canaanite gods were later absorbed into Yahweh as well, such as the storm god Baal (Exodus 15:1-18).

Monarchic Yahwism (930-586 BCE)

The elites in the kingdom of Israel soon endorsed a monolatristic religion, that is, the belief in many gods but the worship of only one. This ancient religion is called Yahwism. Other neighboring kingdoms had their own national gods. Chemosh was the god of Moab. Moloch was the god of the Ammonites. Qaus was the god of the Edomites. While the elites in Israel adopted Yahwism, the general population was still polytheistic.

> All churches and all religions contain aspects of the truth, but only God is truth.
>
> PAT BUCKLEY

In 722 BCE the Kingdom of Israel rebelled against the Assyrian Empire and was subsequently destroyed. Refugees from Israel fled to Judah. With them they brought the religion of Yahwism, and the landowning elites in Judah adopted this religion. In the 7th century BCE, the Judean elites placed eight-year-old Josiah on the throne. During his reign, the Assyrian empire collapsed and Judah experienced a great independence movement. King Josiah led the charge through the launching of a full-scale reform of Yahweh-alone worship and banned the worship of any other god. In 586 BCE, Judah was conquered by the Neo-Babylonian empire (known as the Chaldeans) ruled by Nebuchadnezzar II.

Babylonian Exile (605-538 BCE)

Archaeological evidence suggests that the majority of the population in Judah remained in Judah and continued their customs, while the Judean elites were taken captive to Babylon. The trauma of the exile eventually led to the development of a stronger sense of Hebrew identity within Babylon. As part of their identity, the Judean elites adopted a strict monotheistic theology. This theology would become the inspiration of significant portions of the Hebrew Bible and laid the foundation of Second Temple Judaism. By the end of the Babylonian exile, the existence of other gods was denied by the Hebrews, and Yahweh became the only true God of the world.

Second Temple Judaism (538 BCE-70 CE)

In 539 BCE, the Persian army conquered Babylon under the leadership of Cyrus the Great. A year later, Cyrus made a public declaration that allowed the exiled Jews to return to Jerusalem. When the exiles returned, they re-established themselves as the ruling elite. They very quickly implemented their new monotheistic religion. This was the beginning of Second Temple Judaism. Much of the modern Hebrew Bible was assembled during this time. Old scriptures were revised and edited and new scriptures were added to advocate for a stricter monotheism. These scriptures include the Torah, the histories, and the prophetic and wisdom literature. New concepts of priesthood, a new emphasis on the sacredness of the written law, the prohibition of uttering Yahweh's sacred name, and the banning of intermarriage between Jews and non-Jews were established. Various schools of theology developed within Second Temple Judaism, including the Pharisees, Sadducees, Essenes, Samaritanism, and smaller messianic movements.

It has been hypothesized that the Hebrew transition from monolatristicism (the belief in many gods but the worship of only one) to monotheism (the belief in only one god) was strongly influenced by the Persian religion of Zoroastrianism. Zoroastrianism is arguably the world's first monotheistic

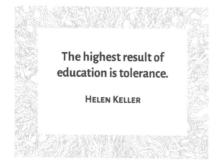

The highest result of education is tolerance.

HELEN KELLER

religion. Several concepts in Second Temple Judaism are identical in Zoroastrianism. One of these is the concept of the last judgment. Zoroastrians believed that there would be a final renovation of the universe, an event Zoroastrians called Frashokereti, where Angra Mainyu (destructive spirit) would be destroyed by Ahura Mazda (God). The story of Satan's defeat in the last days and the restoration of the world at the hands of Yahweh is a clear parallel of this Zoroastrian story. After its adoption into Judaism, apocalyptic literature became extremely popular, setting the stage for a future Messiah to become King of a new world. Jesus became the Messiah many were hoping for.

Apostolic Age (30-100 CE)

After Jesus' death, the belief that he was the hoped-for Messiah spread across the Jewish world thanks to the work of his apostles. The earliest Christian converts were apocalyptic Jewish Christians. Saul of Tarsus, a Roman and a Jew, persecuted these Jewish Christians. After his mystical conversion on the road to Damascus, however, he came to revere Jesus as the Christ. He immediately stopped persecuting Christians and began his own ministry. He focused mainly on proselytizing to the Gentile population. This presented a major problem for the Jewish-Christian leaders. The Gentiles, being non-Jews, did not observe the Jewish law. Paul argued that a Christian did not have to observe the Jewish law and that faith in Christ was enough. Though his views were combated by the other apostles, Paul's teachings spread like wildfire. Under his authority, many in

> Tolerance implies no lack of commitment to one's own beliefs. Rather, it condemns the oppression or persecution of others.
>
> JOHN F. KENNEDY

the Greek world became Christians. With the majority of Christian converts being Gentiles, Paul's theology would come to dominate mainstream Christian thought for the next two thousand years.

Ante-Nicene Period and Late Antiquity (100-476 CE)

The Ante-Nicene Period covered the period between the Apostolic Age and the First Council of Nicaea. It was a time of great diversity within Christianity. There were a vast number of Christian sects throughout the world, each having their own beliefs and practices. Church leaders within these differing sects were fiercely divided, and this soon got the attention of the Roman Emperor who intended to keep his empire unified.

In 313 CE, Emperor Constantine I issued the Edict of Milan, which officially legalized Christian worship. He knew that Christians made up a good portion of his empire and their numbers were growing. To keep their support and a unified empire, he converted to Christianity and began to financially support the church. He built churches, granted special privileges to clergymen, and promoted Christians to high political offices. He intended to bring together the top church leaders in the world and come up with a unified Christian theology. At the First Council of Nicaea in 325, Constantine helped formulate the first unified doctrines of the church. Fifty-five years later, Emperor Theodosius issued the Edict of Thessalonica, which made Christianity the state religion of Rome. Subsequent Church Councils added additional doctrines and declared any doctrines outside of the collective agreement as heresy.

In 476, Rome fell to the Germanic tribes, sending Europe into the Dark Ages.

The Dark Ages (5th-16th centuries)

Despite the fall of the Christianized Roman Empire, Christianity continued to expand globally, evolving into new forms with every culture it encountered. In the 5th century, leaders of all the churches came together to canonize the Bible. The majority of lay Christians were illiterate, however, and they relied heavily on learned church leaders to guide them in Christian living.

In the 8th and 9th centuries, Charles Charlemagne established schools to address the problems of illiteracy. The Carolingian Renaissance brought an intellectual and cultural revival in literature and the arts to the West. Four centuries later, the Italian Renaissance reintroduced the classical literature of Ancient Greece and Rome. Medieval culture continued to change, and in the 16th century the Protestant Reformation led to a vast reformation in Christian understanding. Accompanied by Johannes Gutenberg's invention of the printing press and the rising literacy rates, the Protestant Reformation inspired many Christians to distance themselves from the 1500 year-old Catholic Church and put sole reliance on the Bible as the ultimate authority for Christian living.

Modern Christianity (16th Century- 20th Century)

Modern Christianity saw an emergence of new Christian denominations, each with their own doctrines and interpretations of the Bible. At the same time, new breakthroughs in science, such as Galileo's reintroduction of Copernicus' theory of a heliocentric universe, caused Christianity to adjust. In response to the changing perspectives, the Catholic Church initiated major reforms aimed at expanding their influence. These included anti-corruption measures and the establishment of seminaries and new religious orders. Catholic nations soon took the lead in the Age of Exploration between the 15th and the 17th

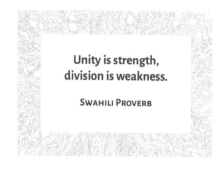

Unity is strength,
division is weakness.

SWAHILI PROVERB

centuries. Their ultimate goal was to spread their version of Christianity to all populations throughout the world. Protestants also joined in the Age of Exploration and in the expansion of their theologies. This was especially evident in the English colonies, where Protestant ideals were emphasized. Colonialism made Christianity a true global religion.

From the 17th century onward, capitalism, rationalism, and science dominated the Western mind. With these newfound values, Christianity became less and less a dominant philosophy. In response to the receding faith, men like Jonathan Edwards and George Whitfield led what would become a new religious revival called the Great Awakening with an emphasis on the personal connection with God. Denominations such as Congregationalist, Presbyterian, Baptist, and Methodist arose from this revival. Subsequent Great Awakenings and revivals inspired the rise of new denominations and movements, including the Holiness Movement and the Restoration Movement.

The 19th and 20th centuries saw the publication of Charles Darwin's theory of evolution, the ending of slavery, the rise of feminism, the Civil Rights Movement, and the introduction of Eastern religions and philosophies into the West. Colonial Christianity's influence waned in the West due to its inability to adapt to and evolve with the ever changing cultures of America and Europe. In response, new liberal denominations emerged in an attempt to make Christianity relevant to the modern world.

Postmodern Christianity (21st Century)

Today, we live in the era of globalization. The sharing of ideas has expanded significantly thanks to the invention of the internet. We have much greater access today to a plethora of information and are able to learn about a wide variety of people from a wide variety of different cultures. New spiritual conversations are happening between the various religious traditions, and Christianity is at a major crossroads moving forward.

The Great Commission: The Call to Spiritual Awakening

Let us revisit Jesus' call to his disciples before his ascension.

> *Then the eleven disciples went to Galilee, to the mountain where Jesus had told them to go. When they saw him, they worshiped him; but some doubted. Then Jesus came to them and said, "All authority in heaven and on earth has been given to me. Therefore go and make disciples of all nations, baptizing them in the name of the Father and of the Son and of the Holy Spirit, and teaching them to obey everything I have commanded you. And surely I am with you always, to the very end of the age." (Matthew 28:16-20)*

Note that Jesus never said to convert the world to Christianity. Jesus said go out and make disciples of every nation and teach them to obey his commandments. What commandments was he referring to? Jesus summed up his commandments six chapters earlier:

> *'Love the Lord your God with all your heart and with all your soul and with all your mind.' This is the first and greatest commandment. And the second is like it: 'Love your neighbor as yourself.' All the Law and the Prophets hang on these two commandments. (Matthew 22:36-40)*

The Great Commission is not to make more Christians: the Great Commission is to make disciples of love. That *is* the Christian identity, at least if we claim to follow Jesus.

Unlike the perspectives of many of the authors in the Old Testament, Jesus understood diversity. He was tolerant and accepting of people very different from himself. He spent much of his ministry with different people which included the Samaritans, the Greeks, the Romans, the tax collectors, the prostitutes, the demon-possessed, the disabled, and the sick. He refused to curse others when asked to by his religious followers, declaring that whoever was not against him was for him (Luke 9:52-56). He believed his message applied to all people, no matter their religion or their culture. Jesus introduced us to the Christ he was, a Christ who was before all time and that is within all creation, including every human being. As Paul reiterated to the Corinthians:

> Just as a body, though one, has many parts, but all its many parts form one body, so it is with Christ. For we were all baptized by one Spirit so as to form one body- whether Jews or Gentiles, slave or free- and we were all given the one Spirit to drink. Even so the body is not made up of one part but of many.
>
> Now if the foot should say, "Because I am not a hand, I do not belong to the body," it would not for that reason stop being part of the body. And if the ear should say, "Because I am not an eye, I do not belong to the body," it would not for that reason stop being part of the body. If the whole body were an eye, where would the sense of hearing be? If the whole body were an ear, where would the sense of smell be? But in fact God has placed the parts in the body, every one of them, just as he wanted them to be. If they were all one part, where would the body be? As it is, there are many parts, but one body. (1 Corinthians 12)

God has placed the parts of the body where God wanted them to be. The body of Christ is not merely the Christian body; the body of Christ is the entire body of humanity. How beautiful it would be for a Christian to gather at God's table with a Buddhist, a Hindu, and/or a Muslim! How beautiful it would be to explore the various human expressions of God together, putting our egos aside and being driven by love. How beautiful it would be to delve into the Christ consciousness of love that is already within each of us and make others aware of this same Christ consciousness that lies within them. This is the Great Commission: to awaken that Christ consciousness within humanity. Some awakened individuals will choose Christianity. Great! Some will choose Islam. Awesome! Others will choose Eastern religions such as Hinduism and Buddhism. Sweet! While all religions are limited, Christ is boundless. While all religions change over time, Christ is the same yesterday, today, and forever. While all religions are temporary, Christ is eternal. Our responsibility as Christians, who claim to follow Jesus, is to lead the way to Christ through love.

The Human Ecosystem

We are all part of the human ecosystem. In the human ecosystem are various trees, shrubs, and grasses, each planted into the Ground of Being. From the Ground of Being comes life. When a plant is separated from the Ground, it loses its life-force and dies. Plants that remain rooted in the Ground stay alive and grow.

> Every individual is a unique manifestation of the Whole, as every branch is a particular outreaching of the tree.
>
> **ALAN WATTS**

Few of us are trees, whose roots grow deep into the Ground. The trees are the great spiritual founders of the major world religions. Just as there are various trees, there are various teachers. When a tree is uprooted and placed on a pedestal to only be worshiped, it loses its life force. The same happens if a tree is cut down to be used for selfish ambition. The tree is meant to be rooted into the Ground. Under each tree grows smaller trees, shrubs and grasses. The smaller trees are the mystics who have understood the messages of the great spiritual founders and rooted themselves deeply in the same Ground where they are continuously fed. Then there are shrubs and grasses, which have narrow roots. These are the followers of the world religions that value their location underneath their respective trees but have limited interest in growing their roots further into the Ground.

The beauty and health of the entire human ecosystem lies in the diversity of its plants. As Christians, we live in an ecosystem under the tree of Jesus. Some of us live his teaching, becoming deeply rooted into the Ground ourselves and establish ourselves as smaller trees in the system of Christianity. Many of us are shrubs and grasses, relying on the shade of Jesus to protect us from the struggles of life but have little interest in growing into trees ourselves.

The tree of Jesus lives amongst other great trees, each with their own systems of smaller trees, shrubs, and grasses. Every plant and combination makes up the entire spiritual ecosystem.

A Call for Tolerance and Collaboration

It is time for Christians to elevate their consciousness and begin to see other religions and philosophies as potential ways for people to connect to the Divine.

Converting others to Christianity is not the Great Commission of Jesus. Jesus never preached hatred towards other religions. Jesus left us with the instruction to love as he loved and spread that love wherever and to whomever we can. To do this, we must have tolerance of others' beliefs. Tolerance does not mean you need to sacrifice your own beliefs. As former president John F. Kennedy once said:

> **Oneness is the absolute truth; duality is an illusion.**
>
> SHRADHA SHUKLA

Tolerance implies no lack of commitment to one's own beliefs. Rather, it condemns the oppression or persecution of others.

Tolerance is the ability to value people in their unique expressions and to see them as part of the human story to understand God. If we can transcend our religious egotism, respect one another in our differences, and aim to work collaboratively in the spiritual awakening of the world, we will fulfill the calling of the Great Commission.

Reflection | *Questions*

1. Does any religion have a right to make a sole claim of God?

    _____

    _____

    _____

    _____

    _____

    _____

2. If I have a fear of other religions, where did this fear come from?

    _____

    _____

    _____

    _____

    _____

    _____

3. How has intolerance affected my relationships with others?

_____

_____

_____

_____

_____

_____

_____

4. How can being more tolerant of and working with others help fulfill the Great Commission?

_____

_____

_____

_____

_____

_____

_____

Prayer   *Practice*

On a piece of paper write down as many religions as you can think of. Then circle the religions you have a tough time accepting.

While in your prayer practice, ask yourself: Why do I have a tough time accepting *this* religion? Observe your thoughts and your emotions. Then ask yourself: How can I be more loving towards these religions? Again, observe your thoughts and emotions. Finally, meditate on the following verse:

> And [Jesus] sent messengers on ahead, who went into a Samaritan village to get things ready for him; but the people there did not welcome him, because he was heading for Jerusalem. When the disciples James and John saw this, they asked, "Lord, do you want us to call fire down from heaven to destroy them?" But Jesus turned and rebuked them. (Luke 9:52-55)

Epilogue

And so we come back to the beginning, to the much-used but minimally emphasized statement that has inspired the writing of this book: Christianity is not about religion; it is about relationship.

I am so glad you decided to journey with me through this provocative but hopefully transformative work. My greatest hope is that this book has given you an insight that will help you along your spiritual voyage.

I hope this book has reassured you that there are more out there like you. I remember being a lone wanderer on the Christian mystical path. For years I searched for others like me who sought God alone and committed to following God even if that means leaving religion behind. It was not until I began to speak my truth that I began to see the need to write a book that could encourage others in their spiritual journey. Surprisingly, many of the positive responses I received regarding the contents expressed in this book were from evangelical, church-going Christians. I then realized that I was not alone in my desire for a trans-religious relationship with God. If you are one who likewise feels drawn to know God beyond religion, I hope this book has encouraged you and given you reassurance that it is okay to engage in such a pursuit. If you continue to seek God, I promise you that your relationship with God will deepen and the fruits of the Spirit will emerge and grow in your life.

It is time for a post-modern and a post-religious Christianity to emerge in Western society. With Jesus' message of love at its core, relationship-based Christianity can become a viable and powerful option for spiritual seekers.

I pray, first and foremost, that you continue to grow in your relationship with God. I pray your spiritual fervor unleashes and no manmade boundaries are able to hold you back. I pray you transcend the perceived notion of a fixed Christianity and find the God that is beyond all religion. I pray that God helps you as you undergo the mindset shifts presented in this book. I pray that you rediscover who you really are as a unique vessel of God's expression. I pray you begin to radiate the love that God is through loving others, as Jesus commanded. I pray that you find God not only in the seen but also in the unseen, in the emptiness between the concepts that attempt to identify God. I pray that you become liberated from everything restricting you, and that through this liberation you are transformed in Christlikeness. I pray that you begin to see sin not as a deliberate act of disobedience but as an opportunity to mend broken fences and grow in Godly love. I pray that you become liberated from fear and remain open to be continuously transformed by God. I pray that you have faith as you enter the unknown parts of life, remaining confident that "all things work together for the good". I pray for an urgency within your soul to better steward the world, to be present here and now and find and express God everywhere and in everything and everyone. I pray that the living Word speaks to you wherever you are, in whatever manifestation the Word decides to take in your life. I pray that you find an assembly of like-minded brothers and sisters that support one another and grow with one another in love. I pray that you work in collaboration with other spiritual seekers, no matter their religious tradition, to bring about a worldwide spiritual awakening.

I love you, my dear friend. Perhaps someday our paths will cross, and if that day comes I will greet you with open arms.

Amen.

About the Author

CODY R. ROTHWELL is a teacher, songwriter, spiritual life coach and Christian mystic. Raised an evangelical Christian, Rothwell underwent a major spiritual transformation in 2010 that led to his embracing the mystical path of Christianity. He has been an advocate of Christian mysticism ever since. Rothwell graduated from Seattle Pacific University with a Bachelor's degree in Social Science Education and was subsequently trained through the John  Maxwell Team as a life coach, leadership trainer, and small group coordinator. He lives in Castle Rock, Washington with his wife Krista and two daughters, Eily and Emerson.